# This Book Belongs To:

____________________________

____________________________

# Addition Practice
## 0-50

1) 11 + 3 = _____    2) 4 + 2 = _____    3) 28 + 9 = _____

4) 1 + 38 = _____    5) 21 + 28 = _____    6) 10 + 29 = _____

7) 47 + 1 = _____    8) 25 + 18 = _____    9) 1 + 47 = _____

10) 43 + 5 = _____    11) 11 + 14 = _____    12) 10 + 19 = _____

13) 17 + 15 = _____    14) 18 + 8 = _____    15) 17 + 27 = _____

16) 18 + 4 = _____    17) 47 + 1 = _____    18) 25 + 5 = _____

19) 38 + 6 = _____    20) 3 + 46 = _____    21) 3 + 27 = _____

22) 3 + 31 = _____    23) 1 + 20 = _____    24) 38 + 4 = _____

25) 3 + 12 = _____    26) 7 + 15 = _____    27) 18 + 18 = _____

28) 5 + 24 = _____    29) 12 + 7 = _____    30) 12 + 11 = _____

31) 32 + 8 = _____    32) 47 + 3 = _____    33) 43 + 3 = _____

34) 40 + 2 = _____    35) 18 + 22 = _____    36) 22 + 24 = _____

37) 46 + 1 = _____    38) 7 + 38 = _____    39) 13 + 0 = _____

40) 13 + 34 = _____    41) 18 + 15 = _____    42) 6 + 42 = _____

43) 11 + 11 = _____    44) 23 + 8 = _____    45) 5 + 14 = _____

1) 36 + 9 = _____   2) 37 + 8 = _____   3) 20 + 26 = _____

4) 27 + 2 = _____   5) 15 + 5 = _____   6) 10 + 33 = _____

7) 43 + 6 = _____   8) 12 + 35 = _____   9) 23 + 26 = _____

10) 33 + 11 = _____   11) 22 + 21 = _____   12) 38 + 11 = _____

13) 30 + 9 = _____   14) 22 + 15 = _____   15) 28 + 13 = _____

16) 8 + 15 = _____   17) 7 + 43 = _____   18) 0 + 50 = _____

19) 30 + 16 = _____   20) 8 + 22 = _____   21) 5 + 34 = _____

22) 3 + 41 = _____   23) 21 + 28 = _____   24) 26 + 18 = _____

25) 1 + 21 = _____   26) 10 + 16 = _____   27) 6 + 31 = _____

28) 10 + 39 = _____   29) 5 + 31 = _____   30) 10 + 24 = _____

31) 14 + 30 = _____   32) 3 + 7 = _____   33) 30 + 18 = _____

34) 31 + 4 = _____   35) 23 + 7 = _____   36) 4 + 41 = _____

37) 0 + 48 = _____   38) 11 + 38 = _____   39) 18 + 25 = _____

40) 5 + 44 = _____   41) 12 + 31 = _____   42) 3 + 6 = _____

43) 6 + 26 = _____   44) 21 + 24 = _____   45) 29 + 4 = _____

1)  26 + 10 = _____      2)  39 + 3 = _____      3)  18 + 30 = _____

4)  5 + 23 = _____       5)  10 + 34 = _____     6)  8 + 41 = _____

7)  33 + 14 = _____      8)  6 + 40 = _____      9)  4 + 16 = _____

10)  16 + 32 = _____     11)  4 + 17 = _____     12)  5 + 45 = _____

13)  22 + 15 = _____     14)  26 + 20 = _____    15)  22 + 19 = _____

16)  2 + 35 = _____      17)  6 + 38 = _____     18)  7 + 0 = _____

19)  4 + 32 = _____      20)  2 + 48 = _____     21)  0 + 50 = _____

22)  23 + 13 = _____     23)  40 + 3 = _____     24)  37 + 3 = _____

25)  11 + 32 = _____     26)  37 + 3 = _____     27)  23 + 19 = _____

28)  32 + 6 = _____      29)  48 + 2 = _____     30)  18 + 24 = _____

31)  13 + 34 = _____     32)  29 + 6 = _____     33)  12 + 17 = _____

34)  17 + 5 = _____      35)  17 + 31 = _____    36)  27 + 22 = _____

37)  47 + 2 = _____      38)  40 + 9 = _____     39)  41 + 7 = _____

40)  38 + 5 = _____      41)  18 + 13 = _____    42)  5 + 27 = _____

43)  1 + 49 = _____      44)  35 + 15 = _____    45)  4 + 45 = _____

| | | |
|---|---|---|
| 1) 7 + 16 = _____ | 2) 10 + 19 = _____ | 3) 1 + 6 = _____ |
| 4) 5 + 29 = _____ | 5) 16 + 15 = _____ | 6) 5 + 40 = _____ |
| 7) 3 + 16 = _____ | 8) 45 + 4 = _____ | 9) 41 + 5 = _____ |
| 10) 5 + 7 = _____ | 11) 20 + 3 = _____ | 12) 3 + 22 = _____ |
| 13) 33 + 17 = _____ | 14) 47 + 2 = _____ | 15) 48 + 1 = _____ |
| 16) 10 + 9 = _____ | 17) 7 + 41 = _____ | 18) 22 + 23 = _____ |
| 19) 49 + 1 = _____ | 20) 2 + 18 = _____ | 21) 6 + 6 = _____ |
| 22) 11 + 6 = _____ | 23) 32 + 16 = _____ | 24) 21 + 24 = _____ |
| 25) 20 + 17 = _____ | 26) 36 + 12 = _____ | 27) 0 + 20 = _____ |
| 28) 22 + 16 = _____ | 29) 20 + 29 = _____ | 30) 44 + 5 = _____ |
| 31) 36 + 9 = _____ | 32) 1 + 20 = _____ | 33) 12 + 23 = _____ |
| 34) 0 + 50 = _____ | 35) 11 + 20 = _____ | 36) 5 + 7 = _____ |
| 37) 37 + 12 = _____ | 38) 17 + 28 = _____ | 39) 30 + 18 = _____ |
| 40) 1 + 26 = _____ | 41) 3 + 45 = _____ | 42) 5 + 19 = _____ |
| 43) 8 + 12 = _____ | 44) 7 + 36 = _____ | 45) 1 + 20 = _____ |

1) 6 + 1 = _____     2) 33 + 2 = _____     3) 34 + 5 = _____

4) 26 + 7 = _____     5) 7 + 27 = _____     6) 28 + 3 = _____

7) 16 + 14 = _____     8) 17 + 7 = _____     9) 29 + 10 = _____

10) 5 + 31 = _____     11) 17 + 28 = _____     12) 28 + 7 = _____

13) 4 + 41 = _____     14) 20 + 27 = _____     15) 9 + 4 = _____

16) 22 + 13 = _____     17) 22 + 5 = _____     18) 14 + 32 = _____

19) 1 + 35 = _____     20) 14 + 23 = _____     21) 4 + 31 = _____

22) 5 + 42 = _____     23) 27 + 7 = _____     24) 3 + 16 = _____

25) 7 + 36 = _____     26) 16 + 9 = _____     27) 5 + 41 = _____

28) 20 + 25 = _____     29) 29 + 7 = _____     30) 35 + 13 = _____

31) 3 + 41 = _____     32) 6 + 23 = _____     33) 8 + 22 = _____

34) 19 + 4 = _____     35) 2 + 48 = _____     36) 7 + 23 = _____

37) 44 + 5 = _____     38) 30 + 19 = _____     39) 11 + 12 = _____

40) 28 + 12 = _____     41) 32 + 11 = _____     42) 11 + 6 = _____

43) 3 + 46 = _____     44) 29 + 2 = _____     45) 42 + 5 = _____

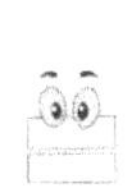

1)  24 + 12 = _____ 2)  2 + 35 = _____ 3)  32 + 17 = _____

4)  48 + 1 = _____ 5)  1 + 47 = _____ 6)  2 + 48 = _____

7)  42 + 4 = _____ 8)  47 + 1 = _____ 9)  8 + 20 = _____

10)  12 + 7 = _____ 11)  33 + 7 = _____ 12)  8 + 7 = _____

13)  42 + 7 = _____ 14)  19 + 28 = _____ 15)  23 + 2 = _____

16)  3 + 41 = _____ 17)  12 + 29 = _____ 18)  9 + 7 = _____

19)  4 + 46 = _____ 20)  49 + 1 = _____ 21)  7 + 31 = _____

22)  2 + 16 = _____ 23)  2 + 23 = _____ 24)  40 + 1 = _____

25)  3 + 23 = _____ 26)  29 + 4 = _____ 27)  44 + 2 = _____

28)  13 + 25 = _____ 29)  1 + 35 = _____ 30)  15 + 18 = _____

31)  2 + 27 = _____ 32)  39 + 5 = _____ 33)  11 + 18 = _____

34)  19 + 14 = _____ 35)  25 + 1 = _____ 36)  8 + 28 = _____

37)  9 + 23 = _____ 38)  1 + 31 = _____ 39)  22 + 0 = _____

40)  28 + 21 = _____ 41)  11 + 20 = _____ 42)  20 + 16 = _____

43)  26 + 24 = _____ 44)  9 + 41 = _____ 45)  34 + 7 = _____

1)  14 + 24 = _____    2)  9 + 25 = _____    3)  30 + 19 = _____

4)  42 + 5 = _____    5)  26 + 10 = _____    6)  27 + 17 = _____

7)  24 + 22 = _____    8)  35 + 15 = _____    9)  4 + 9 = _____

10)  42 + 1 = _____    11)  19 + 5 = _____    12)  2 + 49 = _____

13)  9 + 10 = _____    14)  32 + 4 = _____    15)  6 + 28 = _____

16)  19 + 30 = _____    17)  28 + 3 = _____    18)  2 + 28 = _____

19)  40 + 6 = _____    20)  3 + 38 = _____    21)  2 + 41 = _____

22)  11 + 17 = _____    23)  40 + 7 = _____    24)  7 + 19 = _____

25)  9 + 22 = _____    26)  11 + 19 = _____    27)  19 + 24 = _____

28)  29 + 4 = _____    29)  3 + 46 = _____    30)  13 + 32 = _____

31)  26 + 20 = _____    32)  7 + 15 = _____    33)  5 + 44 = _____

34)  2 + 27 = _____    35)  2 + 31 = _____    36)  2 + 36 = _____

37)  22 + 26 = _____    38)  44 + 3 = _____    39)  21 + 6 = _____

40)  4 + 12 = _____    41)  43 + 4 = _____    42)  5 + 39 = _____

43)  32 + 1 = _____    44)  5 + 35 = _____    45)  41 + 3 = _____

1)  18 + 8 = _____      2)  4 + 39 = _____      3)  36 + 0 = _____

4)  0 + 20 = _____      5)  28 + 12 = _____      6)  23 + 20 = _____

7)  42 + 8 = _____      8)  21 + 29 = _____      9)  40 + 9 = _____

10)  26 + 14 = _____      11)  32 + 16 = _____      12)  21 + 9 = _____

13)  32 + 9 = _____      14)  44 + 6 = _____      15)  14 + 17 = _____

16)  41 + 5 = _____      17)  50 + 0 = _____      18)  42 + 4 = _____

19)  15 + 30 = _____      20)  1 + 30 = _____      21)  6 + 32 = _____

22)  10 + 5 = _____      23)  40 + 1 = _____      24)  27 + 13 = _____

25)  8 + 24 = _____      26)  5 + 19 = _____      27)  35 + 10 = _____

28)  2 + 35 = _____      29)  18 + 27 = _____      30)  8 + 37 = _____

31)  9 + 1 = _____      32)  0 + 50 = _____      33)  46 + 4 = _____

34)  12 + 37 = _____      35)  23 + 4 = _____      36)  2 + 42 = _____

37)  25 + 4 = _____      38)  24 + 17 = _____      39)  42 + 1 = _____

40)  23 + 14 = _____      41)  21 + 2 = _____      42)  30 + 10 = _____

43)  40 + 5 = _____      44)  5 + 42 = _____      45)  18 + 22 = _____

1)  25 + 21 = _____    2)  14 + 26 = _____    3)  23 + 12 = _____

4)  10 + 8 = _____    5)  42 + 6 = _____    6)  8 + 17 = _____

7)  28 + 20 = _____    8)  28 + 17 = _____    9)  0 + 22 = _____

10)  32 + 11 = _____    11)  13 + 17 = _____    12)  12 + 30 = _____

13)  11 + 36 = _____    14)  2 + 36 = _____    15)  28 + 18 = _____

16)  9 + 26 = _____    17)  21 + 11 = _____    18)  28 + 9 = _____

19)  41 + 4 = _____    20)  22 + 27 = _____    21)  32 + 16 = _____

22)  16 + 25 = _____    23)  18 + 31 = _____    24)  1 + 46 = _____

25)  45 + 4 = _____    26)  37 + 5 = _____    27)  11 + 0 = _____

28)  4 + 27 = _____    29)  6 + 37 = _____    30)  40 + 7 = _____

31)  9 + 32 = _____    32)  1 + 49 = _____    33)  1 + 49 = _____

34)  44 + 1 = _____    35)  1 + 49 = _____    36)  2 + 4 = _____

37)  2 + 14 = _____    38)  20 + 14 = _____    39)  11 + 35 = _____

40)  3 + 15 = _____    41)  48 + 2 = _____    42)  1 + 32 = _____

43)  11 + 13 = _____    44)  32 + 10 = _____    45)  4 + 47 = _____

1) 21 + 8 = _____    2) 47 + 1 = _____    3) 26 + 9 = _____

4) 23 + 8 = _____    5) 14 + 0 = _____    6) 1 + 39 = _____

7) 3 + 31 = _____    8) 25 + 3 = _____    9) 1 + 47 = _____

10) 1 + 18 = _____    11) 7 + 15 = _____    12) 4 + 39 = _____

13) 19 + 10 = _____    14) 11 + 10 = _____    15) 46 + 3 = _____

16) 2 + 48 = _____    17) 1 + 47 = _____    18) 28 + 9 = _____

19) 45 + 4 = _____    20) 14 + 19 = _____    21) 32 + 8 = _____

22) 33 + 14 = _____    23) 42 + 6 = _____    24) 28 + 5 = _____

25) 36 + 8 = _____    26) 5 + 31 = _____    27) 26 + 6 = _____

28) 14 + 31 = _____    29) 2 + 39 = _____    30) 3 + 31 = _____

31) 21 + 20 = _____    32) 7 + 41 = _____    33) 34 + 9 = _____

34) 48 + 1 = _____    35) 13 + 34 = _____    36) 7 + 11 = _____

37) 6 + 43 = _____    38) 4 + 35 = _____    39) 50 + 0 = _____

40) 41 + 8 = _____    41) 31 + 10 = _____    42) 8 + 38 = _____

43) 13 + 9 = _____    44) 8 + 37 = _____    45) 34 + 9 = _____

# Addition Practice
## 0-100

1) 25 + 72 = _____

2) 50 + 29 = _____

3) 37 + 10 = _____

4) 60 + 19 = _____

5) 34 + 55 = _____

6) 9 + 73 = _____

7) 2 + 96 = _____

8) 20 + 33 = _____

9) 19 + 35 = _____

10) 42 + 57 = _____

11) 99 + 1 = _____

12) 28 + 8 = _____

13) 90 + 5 = _____

14) 1 + 30 = _____

15) 61 + 5 = _____

16) 14 + 2 = _____

17) 4 + 87 = _____

18) 9 + 35 = _____

19) 55 + 41 = _____

20) 25 + 8 = _____

21) 84 + 1 = _____

22) 8 + 92 = _____

23) 58 + 10 = _____

24) 17 + 38 = _____

25) 29 + 69 = _____

26) 62 + 28 = _____

27) 87 + 13 = _____

28) 27 + 52 = _____

29) 7 + 70 = _____

30) 2 + 92 = _____

31) 38 + 53 = _____

32) 45 + 52 = _____

33) 43 + 5 = _____

34) 29 + 21 = _____

35) 24 + 54 = _____

36) 30 + 62 = _____

37) 53 + 24 = _____

38) 7 + 79 = _____

39) 3 + 88 = _____

40) 43 + 54 = _____

41) 18 + 69 = _____

42) 21 + 61 = _____

43) 62 + 14 = _____

44) 14 + 68 = _____

45) 65 + 19 = _____

1) 54 + 41 = _____     2) 19 + 21 = _____     3) 39 + 38 = _____

4) 24 + 14 = _____     5) 46 + 25 = _____     6) 1 + 75 = _____

7) 21 + 39 = _____     8) 2 + 95 = _____     9) 6 + 68 = _____

10) 65 + 24 = _____     11) 82 + 13 = _____     12) 77 + 23 = _____

13) 52 + 44 = _____     14) 52 + 37 = _____     15) 73 + 26 = _____

16) 67 + 30 = _____     17) 99 + 1 = _____     18) 14 + 43 = _____

19) 23 + 68 = _____     20) 54 + 23 = _____     21) 56 + 30 = _____

22) 27 + 41 = _____     23) 46 + 28 = _____     24) 99 + 0 = _____

25) 31 + 20 = _____     26) 33 + 42 = _____     27) 48 + 31 = _____

28) 40 + 17 = _____     29) 57 + 8 = _____     30) 41 + 37 = _____

31) 5 + 92 = _____     32) 24 + 59 = _____     33) 80 + 6 = _____

34) 49 + 24 = _____     35) 13 + 1 = _____     36) 41 + 24 = _____

37) 42 + 11 = _____     38) 4 + 92 = _____     39) 25 + 66 = _____

40) 9 + 71 = _____     41) 47 + 19 = _____     42) 10 + 71 = _____

43) 13 + 75 = _____     44) 2 + 35 = _____     45) 73 + 24 = _____

1)  30 + 33 = _____     2)  6 + 5 = _____     3)  26 + 57 = _____

4)  87 + 9 = _____     5)  34 + 20 = _____     6)  73 + 10 = _____

7)  64 + 24 = _____     8)  29 + 4 = _____     9)  4 + 53 = _____

10)  3 + 63 = _____     11)  2 + 93 = _____     12)  16 + 55 = _____

13)  67 + 10 = _____     14)  73 + 0 = _____     15)  92 + 5 = _____

16)  95 + 5 = _____     17)  97 + 0 = _____     18)  56 + 20 = _____

19)  59 + 37 = _____     20)  95 + 2 = _____     21)  30 + 54 = _____

22)  56 + 1 = _____     23)  98 + 2 = _____     24)  5 + 91 = _____

25)  14 + 78 = _____     26)  11 + 17 = _____     27)  64 + 25 = _____

28)  8 + 56 = _____     29)  54 + 9 = _____     30)  37 + 15 = _____

31)  58 + 42 = _____     32)  39 + 60 = _____     33)  73 + 26 = _____

34)  25 + 72 = _____     35)  27 + 50 = _____     36)  58 + 41 = _____

37)  59 + 24 = _____     38)  67 + 6 = _____     39)  98 + 1 = _____

40)  19 + 81 = _____     41)  32 + 25 = _____     42)  1 + 98 = _____

43)  87 + 9 = _____     44)  36 + 55 = _____     45)  49 + 25 = _____

1) 9 + 16 = _____        2) 54 + 6 = _____        3) 90 + 1 = _____

4) 50 + 29 = _____       5) 20 + 18 = _____       6) 12 + 88 = _____

7) 9 + 86 = _____        8) 16 + 37 = _____       9) 36 + 15 = _____

10) 70 + 8 = _____       11) 55 + 7 = _____       12) 12 + 76 = _____

13) 22 + 77 = _____      14) 49 + 33 = _____      15) 5 + 87 = _____

16) 3 + 23 = _____       17) 86 + 14 = _____      18) 3 + 52 = _____

19) 21 + 61 = _____      20) 9 + 85 = _____       21) 64 + 5 = _____

22) 75 + 2 = _____       23) 54 + 30 = _____      24) 3 + 91 = _____

25) 6 + 65 = _____       26) 45 + 39 = _____      27) 8 + 7 = _____

28) 58 + 10 = _____      29) 24 + 50 = _____      30) 40 + 30 = _____

31) 61 + 20 = _____      32) 23 + 11 = _____      33) 26 + 13 = _____

34) 42 + 44 = _____      35) 16 + 1 = _____       36) 20 + 29 = _____

37) 13 + 46 = _____      38) 92 + 4 = _____       39) 43 + 24 = _____

40) 20 + 33 = _____      41) 39 + 44 = _____      42) 9 + 60 = _____

43) 61 + 19 = _____      44) 76 + 17 = _____      45) 30 + 28 = _____

1) 21 + 70 = _____ 　　2) 5 + 62 = _____ 　　3) 18 + 40 = _____

4) 58 + 33 = _____ 　　5) 33 + 34 = _____ 　　6) 43 + 11 = _____

7) 15 + 76 = _____ 　　8) 78 + 17 = _____ 　　9) 48 + 46 = _____

10) 90 + 1 = _____ 　　11) 81 + 3 = _____ 　　12) 50 + 24 = _____

13) 15 + 80 = _____ 　　14) 18 + 44 = _____ 　　15) 89 + 10 = _____

16) 30 + 20 = _____ 　　17) 55 + 8 = _____ 　　18) 1 + 79 = _____

19) 23 + 13 = _____ 　　20) 42 + 34 = _____ 　　21) 38 + 39 = _____

22) 2 + 93 = _____ 　　23) 69 + 19 = _____ 　　24) 4 + 90 = _____

25) 87 + 6 = _____ 　　26) 51 + 37 = _____ 　　27) 4 + 83 = _____

28) 46 + 3 = _____ 　　29) 64 + 15 = _____ 　　30) 12 + 34 = _____

31) 66 + 16 = _____ 　　32) 6 + 89 = _____ 　　33) 19 + 71 = _____

34) 82 + 8 = _____ 　　35) 25 + 76 = _____ 　　36) 10 + 56 = _____

37) 42 + 28 = _____ 　　38) 38 + 5 = _____ 　　39) 65 + 3 = _____

40) 44 + 49 = _____ 　　41) 13 + 78 = _____ 　　42) 38 + 39 = _____

43) 17 + 13 = _____ 　　44) 47 + 15 = _____ 　　45) 15 + 21 = _____

1)  26 + 63 = _____     2)  28 + 17 = _____     3)  45 + 5 = _____

4)  27 + 61 = _____     5)  19 + 78 = _____     6)  29 + 33 = _____

7)  54 + 41 = _____     8)  70 + 17 = _____     9)  83 + 10 = _____

10)  3 + 39 = _____     11)  22 + 66 = _____     12)  13 + 44 = _____

13)  47 + 6 = _____     14)  61 + 17 = _____     15)  43 + 42 = _____

16)  38 + 19 = _____     17)  7 + 3 = _____     18)  56 + 4 = _____

19)  3 + 92 = _____     20)  9 + 23 = _____     21)  27 + 35 = _____

22)  21 + 65 = _____     23)  5 + 25 = _____     24)  10 + 32 = _____

25)  23 + 30 = _____     26)  59 + 19 = _____     27)  13 + 75 = _____

28)  15 + 76 = _____     29)  77 + 6 = _____     30)  47 + 16 = _____

31)  19 + 40 = _____     32)  38 + 31 = _____     33)  26 + 24 = _____

34)  52 + 1 = _____     35)  52 + 3 = _____     36)  74 + 3 = _____

37)  28 + 60 = _____     38)  92 + 5 = _____     39)  0 + 32 = _____

40)  77 + 12 = _____     41)  33 + 49 = _____     42)  6 + 77 = _____

43)  96 + 3 = _____     44)  37 + 54 = _____     45)  48 + 12 = _____

1) 11 + 26 = _____     2) 16 + 53 = _____     3) 6 + 92 = _____

4) 96 + 4 = _____      5) 13 + 12 = _____     6) 50 + 46 = _____

7) 96 + 1 = _____      8) 13 + 76 = _____     9) 18 + 70 = _____

10) 15 + 25 = _____    11) 46 + 43 = _____    12) 2 + 94 = _____

13) 81 + 16 = _____    14) 1 + 52 = _____     15) 59 + 38 = _____

16) 30 + 18 = _____    17) 18 + 47 = _____    18) 22 + 22 = _____

19) 51 + 39 = _____    20) 38 + 37 = _____    21) 80 + 10 = _____

22) 35 + 42 = _____    23) 31 + 10 = _____    24) 41 + 57 = _____

25) 80 + 12 = _____    26) 2 + 69 = _____     27) 48 + 2 = _____

28) 73 + 24 = _____    29) 6 + 88 = _____     30) 90 + 4 = _____

31) 20 + 36 = _____    32) 37 + 41 = _____    33) 7 + 78 = _____

34) 34 + 17 = _____    35) 13 + 48 = _____    36) 5 + 15 = _____

37) 73 + 1 = _____     38) 44 + 29 = _____    39) 96 + 2 = _____

40) 50 + 1 = _____     41) 77 + 4 = _____     42) 10 + 18 = _____

43) 81 + 16 = _____    44) 97 + 2 = _____     45) 1 + 89 = _____

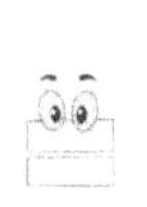

| | | |
|---|---|---|
| 1)  38 + 24 = _____ | 2)  28 + 67 = _____ | 3)  53 + 6 = _____ |
| 4)  3 + 96 = _____ | 5)  50 + 41 = _____ | 6)  68 + 29 = _____ |
| 7)  16 + 75 = _____ | 8)  80 + 5 = _____ | 9)  53 + 31 = _____ |
| 10)  74 + 24 = _____ | 11)  41 + 23 = _____ | 12)  64 + 5 = _____ |
| 13)  81 + 7 = _____ | 14)  2 + 97 = _____ | 15)  3 + 73 = _____ |
| 16)  38 + 32 = _____ | 17)  81 + 8 = _____ | 18)  51 + 6 = _____ |
| 19)  51 + 37 = _____ | 20)  25 + 68 = _____ | 21)  47 + 23 = _____ |
| 22)  90 + 5 = _____ | 23)  41 + 39 = _____ | 24)  28 + 64 = _____ |
| 25)  86 + 6 = _____ | 26)  26 + 53 = _____ | 27)  24 + 53 = _____ |
| 28)  53 + 40 = _____ | 29)  6 + 70 = _____ | 30)  44 + 50 = _____ |
| 31)  1 + 80 = _____ | 32)  24 + 47 = _____ | 33)  22 + 73 = _____ |
| 34)  15 + 59 = _____ | 35)  11 + 16 = _____ | 36)  3 + 27 = _____ |
| 37)  44 + 35 = _____ | 38)  16 + 73 = _____ | 39)  69 + 27 = _____ |
| 40)  97 + 1 = _____ | 41)  5 + 93 = _____ | 42)  10 + 77 = _____ |
| 43)  85 + 9 = _____ | 44)  11 + 85 = _____ | 45)  3 + 65 = _____ |

1) 73 + 15 = _____      2) 29 + 22 = _____      3) 31 + 62 = _____

4) 6 + 19 = _____       5) 67 + 1 = _____       6) 63 + 33 = _____

7) 15 + 36 = _____      8) 76 + 10 = _____      9) 24 + 63 = _____

10) 10 + 79 = _____     11) 11 + 83 = _____     12) 4 + 61 = _____

13) 27 + 54 = _____     14) 19 + 31 = _____     15) 13 + 77 = _____

16) 35 + 3 = _____      17) 43 + 51 = _____     18) 3 + 79 = _____

19) 39 + 8 = _____      20) 6 + 68 = _____      21) 21 + 56 = _____

22) 4 + 82 = _____      23) 18 + 77 = _____     24) 63 + 35 = _____

25) 96 + 1 = _____      26) 10 + 42 = _____     27) 4 + 81 = _____

28) 50 + 33 = _____     29) 41 + 29 = _____     30) 12 + 88 = _____

31) 55 + 0 = _____      32) 11 + 84 = _____     33) 0 + 83 = _____

34) 91 + 9 = _____      35) 78 + 6 = _____      36) 45 + 18 = _____

37) 3 + 91 = _____      38) 4 + 95 = _____      39) 34 + 15 = _____

40) 14 + 41 = _____     41) 48 + 44 = _____     42) 27 + 64 = _____

43) 0 + 83 = _____      44) 50 + 35 = _____     45) 16 + 80 = _____

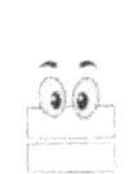

| | | |
|---|---|---|
| 1)  86 + 3 = _____ | 2)  62 + 4 = _____ | 3)  99 + 1 = _____ |
| 4)  45 + 51 = _____ | 5)  8 + 72 = _____ | 6)  20 + 44 = _____ |
| 7)  50 + 27 = _____ | 8)  72 + 12 = _____ | 9)  16 + 74 = _____ |
| 10)  7 + 27 = _____ | 11)  52 + 30 = _____ | 12)  26 + 74 = _____ |
| 13)  76 + 10 = _____ | 14)  7 + 43 = _____ | 15)  93 + 4 = _____ |
| 16)  34 + 28 = _____ | 17)  77 + 16 = _____ | 18)  35 + 15 = _____ |
| 19)  5 + 30 = _____ | 20)  82 + 18 = _____ | 21)  65 + 25 = _____ |
| 22)  1 + 31 = _____ | 23)  85 + 14 = _____ | 24)  88 + 12 = _____ |
| 25)  90 + 8 = _____ | 26)  43 + 12 = _____ | 27)  51 + 34 = _____ |
| 28)  81 + 15 = _____ | 29)  38 + 8 = _____ | 30)  35 + 20 = _____ |
| 31)  23 + 43 = _____ | 32)  20 + 54 = _____ | 33)  4 + 95 = _____ |
| 34)  29 + 6 = _____ | 35)  12 + 11 = _____ | 36)  23 + 8 = _____ |
| 37)  3 + 17 = _____ | 38)  23 + 22 = _____ | 39)  78 + 1 = _____ |
| 40)  50 + 29 = _____ | 41)  48 + 39 = _____ | 42)  70 + 24 = _____ |
| 43)  27 + 46 = _____ | 44)  27 + 71 = _____ | 45)  64 + 34 = _____ |

# Missing Number 0-50

1)  $1 + 36 = \underline{\quad}$

2)  $27 + \underline{\quad} = 50$

3)  $47 + \underline{\quad} = 49$

4)  $\underline{\quad} + 9 = 46$

5)  $15 + 24 = \underline{\quad}$

6)  $14 + \underline{\quad} = 19$

7)  $22 + 13 = \underline{\quad}$

8)  $\underline{\quad} + 15 = 27$

9)  $\underline{\quad} + 9 = 32$

10)  $43 + \underline{\quad} = 50$

11)  $46 + 2 = \underline{\quad}$

12)  $\underline{\quad} + 45 = 49$

13)  $24 + 5 = \underline{\quad}$

14)  $18 + 26 = \underline{\quad}$

15)  $18 + \underline{\quad} = 21$

16)  $\underline{\quad} + 19 = 45$

17)  $\underline{\quad} + 16 = 22$

18)  $16 + 27 = \underline{\quad}$

19)  $1 + \underline{\quad} = 10$

20)  $\underline{\quad} + 37 = 50$

21)  $25 + \underline{\quad} = 36$

22)  $\underline{\quad} + 9 = 48$

23)  $\underline{\quad} + 4 = 46$

24)  $24 + \underline{\quad} = 29$

25)  $34 + 6 = \underline{\quad}$

26)  $\underline{\quad} + 3 = 47$

27)  $11 + \underline{\quad} = 25$

28)  $\underline{\quad} + 18 = 36$

29)  $\underline{\quad} + 1 = 32$

30)  $\underline{\quad} + 50 = 50$

31)  $4 + \underline{\quad} = 47$

32)  $16 + 25 = \underline{\quad}$

33)  $15 + \underline{\quad} = 32$

34)  $13 + 26 = \underline{\quad}$

35)  $\underline{\quad} + 24 = 45$

36)  $33 + \underline{\quad} = 34$

37)  $\underline{\quad} + 23 = 42$

38)  $34 + \underline{\quad} = 50$

39)  $\underline{\quad} + 36 = 44$

40)  $\underline{\quad} + 40 = 47$

41)  $33 + \underline{\quad} = 49$

42)  $\underline{\quad} + 17 = 25$

43)  $\underline{\quad} + 3 = 17$

44)  $\underline{\quad} + 34 = 38$

45)  $30 + \underline{\quad} = 49$

1) _____ + 27 = 28      2) 2 + _____ = 48      3) 40 + _____ = 46

4) _____ + 0 = 48      5) 24 + 12 = _____      6) 3 + _____ = 27

7) _____ + 28 = 47      8) 27 + _____ = 48      9) _____ + 14 = 49

10) 2 + _____ = 50      11) _____ + 48 = 49      12) 1 + 42 = _____

13) _____ + 2 = 36      14) 4 + _____ = 30      15) _____ + 14 = 43

16) 9 + _____ = 18      17) _____ + 22 = 47      18) _____ + 38 = 42

19) _____ + 33 = 45      20) 12 + _____ = 28      21) 41 + 3 = _____

22) _____ + 29 = 38      23) 20 + _____ = 43      24) _____ + 40 = 41

25) 8 + 24 = _____      26) _____ + 36 = 44      27) 36 + 4 = _____

28) 7 + _____ = 9      29) _____ + 4 = 47      30) _____ + 43 = 50

31) 17 + 31 = _____      32) _____ + 3 = 24      33) 25 + 3 = _____

34) _____ + 20 = 25      35) 2 + _____ = 23      36) 27 + 4 = _____

37) _____ + 9 = 49      38) _____ + 25 = 35      39) 5 + _____ = 16

40) 9 + _____ = 26      41) 13 + _____ = 44      42) _____ + 6 = 50

43) 32 + _____ = 48      44) 27 + 1 = _____      45) 11 + _____ = 18

1) _____ + 6 = 42

2) 17 + _____ = 43

3) _____ + 25 = 26

4) _____ + 18 = 23

5) _____ + 10 = 24

6) 41 + _____ = 49

7) 17 + 32 = _____

8) 5 + _____ = 31

9) 5 + _____ = 50

10) _____ + 10 = 43

11) 5 + _____ = 31

12) _____ + 0 = 31

13) 20 + _____ = 23

14) _____ + 27 = 48

15) _____ + 4 = 44

16) 0 + _____ = 23

17) 34 + _____ = 39

18) 4 + 3 = _____

19) _____ + 26 = 38

20) 5 + _____ = 35

21) 0 + _____ = 50

22) 25 + _____ = 47

23) _____ + 43 = 49

24) _____ + 1 = 44

25) 19 + _____ = 24

26) _____ + 4 = 7

27) 16 + 17 = _____

28) _____ + 22 = 32

29) 45 + _____ = 48

30) 20 + _____ = 39

31) _____ + 17 = 17

32) _____ + 20 = 37

33) _____ + 39 = 43

34) _____ + 1 = 49

35) 3 + 46 = _____

36) _____ + 4 = 42

37) 7 + 10 = _____

38) 2 + _____ = 33

39) 3 + _____ = 4

40) _____ + 49 = 50

41) 25 + _____ = 48

42) 4 + 33 = _____

43) _____ + 4 = 32

44) _____ + 8 = 15

45) _____ + 2 = 26

1)  15 + _____ = 45      2) _____ + 26 = 35      3) _____ + 45 = 46

4) _____ + 8 = 21      5)  2 + 15 = _____      6) _____ + 10 = 42

7)  1 + _____ = 45      8) _____ + 24 = 42      9)  16 + _____ = 37

10)  9 + _____ = 35      11)  1 + _____ = 48      12) _____ + 1 = 45

13)  24 + _____ = 38      14)  23 + 9 = _____      15)  17 + 8 = _____

16) _____ + 1 = 50      17) _____ + 4 = 11      18)  3 + _____ = 26

19)  0 + 50 = _____      20) _____ + 32 = 41      21)  21 + 7 = _____

22)  19 + _____ = 45      23)  6 + _____ = 40      24)  19 + _____ = 45

25)  27 + _____ = 31      26)  24 + _____ = 33      27)  13 + 13 = _____

28) _____ + 15 = 46      29) _____ + 20 = 21      30) _____ + 3 = 40

31) _____ + 5 = 32      32)  25 + 18 = _____      33)  34 + _____ = 38

34) _____ + 13 = 41      35)  30 + 16 = _____      36) _____ + 7 = 50

37) _____ + 4 = 49      38)  7 + _____ = 28      39) _____ + 25 = 47

40)  4 + 36 = _____      41) _____ + 19 = 34      42)  38 + _____ = 49

43) _____ + 24 = 41      44)  9 + _____ = 50      45) _____ + 16 = 40

1)  9 + _____ = 45          2)  11 + _____ = 12          3)  4 + _____ = 16

4)  6 + 27 = _____          5)  _____ + 18 = 41          6)  23 + 25 = _____

7)  7 + 4 = _____           8)  _____ + 2 = 11           9)  _____ + 22 = 49

10)  29 + _____ = 35        11)  6 + _____ = 25          12)  _____ + 4 = 38

13)  _____ + 14 = 38        14)  _____ + 11 = 17         15)  33 + _____ = 46

16)  11 + _____ = 25        17)  _____ + 13 = 30         18)  _____ + 41 = 49

19)  1 + _____ = 26         20)  11 + _____ = 18         21)  _____ + 1 = 50

22)  38 + _____ = 39        23)  10 + 34 = _____         24)  _____ + 45 = 46

25)  _____ + 3 = 6          26)  _____ + 31 = 32         27)  33 + _____ = 48

28)  15 + 32 = _____        29)  15 + _____ = 32         30)  _____ + 15 = 17

31)  50 + _____ = 50        32)  _____ + 35 = 45         33)  _____ + 2 = 35

34)  1 + 49 = _____         35)  13 + _____ = 41         36)  1 + 2 = _____

37)  1 + _____ = 39         38)  _____ + 46 = 50         39)  21 + _____ = 25

40)  12 + _____ = 14        41)  25 + 8 = _____          42)  1 + 42 = _____

43)  13 + _____ = 48        44)  _____ + 23 = 49         45)  7 + _____ = 34

1) 40 + _____ = 43     2) 2 + _____ = 2     3) 23 + 10 = _____

4) 17 + _____ = 40     5) _____ + 1 = 34     6) _____ + 4 = 14

7) 9 + 18 = _____     8) _____ + 41 = 45     9) _____ + 11 = 38

10) 14 + _____ = 44     11) 4 + _____ = 33     12) 46 + 0 = _____

13) _____ + 17 = 35     14) 4 + _____ = 25     15) 25 + _____ = 35

16) 42 + 8 = _____     17) 17 + _____ = 45     18) 40 + 2 = _____

19) _____ + 2 = 49     20) 39 + _____ = 39     21) _____ + 14 = 46

22) 45 + _____ = 47     23) 40 + _____ = 41     24) 1 + 49 = _____

25) _____ + 11 = 44     26) _____ + 14 = 24     27) 5 + _____ = 22

28) 2 + 36 = _____     29) 20 + _____ = 33     30) _____ + 5 = 18

31) _____ + 36 = 50     32) 38 + _____ = 47     33) _____ + 10 = 41

34) _____ + 9 = 42     35) _____ + 13 = 47     36) 9 + _____ = 37

37) 5 + 41 = _____     38) 0 + _____ = 35     39) _____ + 7 = 9

40) 16 + _____ = 17     41) 27 + 13 = _____     42) 17 + _____ = 45

43) _____ + 27 = 32     44) 7 + _____ = 43     45) 0 + 50 = _____

1)  _____ + 15 = 33

2)  _____ + 47 = 49

3)  _____ + 23 = 45

4)  14 + 13 = _____

5)  26 + _____ = 44

6)  5 + _____ = 11

7)  _____ + 2 = 50

8)  8 + _____ = 38

9)  _____ + 2 = 41

10)  19 + 7 = _____

11)  16 + 33 = _____

12)  7 + _____ = 44

13)  10 + _____ = 39

14)  _____ + 19 = 47

15)  5 + _____ = 44

16)  25 + 8 = _____

17)  _____ + 46 = 48

18)  _____ + 27 = 51

19)  14 + 31 = _____

20)  _____ + 1 = 47

21)  _____ + 3 = 48

22)  5 + 38 = _____

23)  21 + _____ = 27

24)  6 + _____ = 36

25)  _____ + 21 = 28

26)  1 + _____ = 49

27)  _____ + 1 = 38

28)  48 + _____ = 50

29)  8 + _____ = 46

30)  35 + 8 = _____

31)  12 + _____ = 38

32)  9 + _____ = 41

33)  _____ + 20 = 48

34)  36 + _____ = 48

35)  4 + _____ = 50

36)  13 + _____ = 34

37)  10 + _____ = 45

38)  _____ + 33 = 44

39)  _____ + 13 = 39

40)  14 + _____ = 24

41)  2 + _____ = 27

42)  _____ + 26 = 48

43)  1 + _____ = 24

44)  _____ + 10 = 47

45)  _____ + 16 = 31

1) _____ + 25 = 27        2) 9 + _____ = 31        3) 4 + _____ = 29

4) _____ + 40 = 43        5) 0 + _____ = 4        6) 1 + _____ = 49

7) 10 + 31 = _____        8) 22 + _____ = 33        9) _____ + 38 = 47

10) 5 + _____ = 36        11) _____ + 4 = 36        12) 21 + 24 = _____

13) 36 + _____ = 38        14) _____ + 22 = 35        15) 3 + _____ = 50

16) 37 + _____ = 49        17) _____ + 17 = 48        18) _____ + 15 = 25

19) _____ + 17 = 32        20) 15 + _____ = 29        21) 8 + 11 = _____

22) 2 + _____ = 45        23) 18 + 21 = _____        24) 49 + _____ = 51

25) _____ + 37 = 48        26) _____ + 21 = 24        27) 22 + _____ = 43

28) 20 + _____ = 46        29) 43 + _____ = 46        30) _____ + 4 = 49

31) 8 + 23 = _____        32) 24 + _____ = 25        33) _____ + 33 = 35

34) _____ + 15 = 24        35) _____ + 48 = 50        36) 6 + _____ = 41

37) 9 + 17 = _____        38) 5 + _____ = 46        39) 16 + 32 = _____

40) _____ + 25 = 47        41) 36 + _____ = 47        42) 25 + _____ = 31

43) _____ + 3 = 24        44) 4 + _____ = 40        45) 20 + _____ = 27

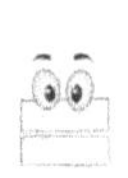

1) 26 + _____ = 45        2) _____ + 13 = 37        3) _____ + 42 = 43

4) 16 + _____ = 41        5) 8 + _____ = 40        6) 49 + 0 = _____

7) _____ + 12 = 26        8) _____ + 7 = 39        9) _____ + 18 = 37

10) 2 + 48 = _____        11) _____ + 15 = 49        12) _____ + 24 = 46

13) _____ + 46 = 48        14) _____ + 5 = 47        15) _____ + 17 = 36

16) 35 + _____ = 40        17) 5 + _____ = 22        18) 3 + 35 = _____

19) 10 + 35 = _____        20) 0 + _____ = 48        21) 3 + 40 = _____

22) 21 + 13 = _____        23) 3 + _____ = 19        24) 26 + _____ = 50

25) 14 + _____ = 27        26) 13 + _____ = 17        27) 24 + _____ = 42

28) _____ + 27 = 40        29) 46 + _____ = 51        30) 34 + _____ = 45

31) _____ + 15 = 16        32) 8 + 32 = _____        33) 27 + _____ = 37

34) _____ + 13 = 27        35) 26 + 7 = _____        36) 1 + _____ = 37

37) 11 + _____ = 17        38) 36 + _____ = 48        39) 1 + _____ = 27

40) 33 + _____ = 37        41) _____ + 40 = 41        42) 1 + _____ = 23

43) _____ + 9 = 16        44) _____ + 2 = 49        45) 25 + 12 = _____

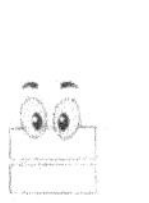

1) 39 + _____ = 43    2) _____ + 29 = 41    3) 22 + 24 = _____

4) 25 + 23 = _____    5) _____ + 2 = 20    6) _____ + 43 = 48

7) 28 + _____ = 50    8) _____ + 37 = 44    9) 24 + _____ = 37

10) 19 + 3 = _____    11) 18 + 3 = _____    12) 2 + 48 = _____

13) _____ + 48 = 49    14) 19 + _____ = 45    15) 1 + _____ = 47

16) 9 + _____ = 39    17) _____ + 35 = 46    18) 3 + _____ = 16

19) 2 + _____ = 50    20) 22 + _____ = 48    21) _____ + 8 = 28

22) 16 + _____ = 17    23) 26 + _____ = 48    24) _____ + 34 = 35

25) 42 + _____ = 50    26) _____ + 11 = 17    27) _____ + 15 = 46

28) 39 + 10 = _____    29) _____ + 8 = 41    30) _____ + 28 = 49

31) 28 + _____ = 35    32) _____ + 44 = 46    33) 20 + 20 = _____

34) _____ + 20 = 42    35) 11 + _____ = 17    36) 24 + _____ = 40

37) _____ + 7 = 36    38) 3 + 44 = _____    39) _____ + 28 = 50

40) 10 + 29 = _____    41) 13 + _____ = 15    42) _____ + 3 = 15

43) 0 + _____ = 48    44) 45 + _____ = 48    45) _____ + 24 = 32

# Missing Number
# 0-100

1) _____ + 38 = 88

2) _____ + 49 = 64

3) 9 + 41 = _____

4) 29 + _____ = 67

5) 54 + _____ = 59

6) _____ + 25 = 56

7) _____ + 67 = 81

8) 3 + _____ = 46

9) 37 + _____ = 41

10) 31 + _____ = 88

11) _____ + 63 = 75

12) _____ + 75 = 82

13) _____ + 15 = 85

14) 1 + _____ = 29

15) _____ + 16 = 89

16) 100 + 0 = _____

17) _____ + 5 = 84

18) _____ + 96 = 97

19) _____ + 0 = 68

20) _____ + 28 = 83

21) _____ + 68 = 89

22) 3 + _____ = 31

23) _____ + 67 = 71

24) _____ + 1 = 39

25) 0 + _____ = 90

26) 3 + _____ = 85

27) 15 + _____ = 97

28) 16 + _____ = 65

29) _____ + 9 = 89

30) 24 + 53 = _____

31) 96 + 2 = _____

32) 59 + _____ = 59

33) 51 + 41 = _____

34) 55 + _____ = 82

35) _____ + 56 = 83

36) 16 + _____ = 34

37) _____ + 56 = 77

38) 79 + _____ = 94

39) 58 + _____ = 99

40) _____ + 13 = 60

41) 34 + _____ = 68

42) _____ + 23 = 79

43) 72 + 2 = _____

44) 28 + _____ = 87

45) _____ + 31 = 88

1) _____ + 1 = 62

2) 83 + _____ = 98

3) 65 + _____ = 69

4) _____ + 97 = 99

5) _____ + 43 = 70

6) 75 + _____ = 87

7) 1 + _____ = 95

8) _____ + 57 = 75

9) _____ + 46 = 85

10) 14 + _____ = 46

11) 18 + _____ = 90

12) _____ + 5 = 75

13) _____ + 31 = 71

14) _____ + 12 = 89

15) _____ + 5 = 70

16) _____ + 21 = 89

17) _____ + 1 = 72

18) _____ + 37 = 72

19) _____ + 34 = 43

20) _____ + 13 = 89

21) 54 + _____ = 98

22) _____ + 24 = 83

23) _____ + 18 = 93

24) 68 + 30 = _____

25) 31 + 58 = _____

26) 32 + 61 = _____

27) 6 + _____ = 11

28) 36 + 9 = _____

29) 14 + _____ = 58

30) 24 + _____ = 58

31) 95 + 4 = _____

32) 9 + _____ = 96

33) _____ + 26 = 82

34) 40 + 55 = _____

35) 22 + 73 = _____

36) 66 + _____ = 91

37) _____ + 5 = 82

38) _____ + 20 = 87

39) 19 + 28 = _____

40) 35 + 6 = _____

41) _____ + 62 = 100

42) 91 + _____ = 97

43) 3 + 46 = _____

44) 71 + 29 = _____

45) 91 + _____ = 95

1)  96 + _____ = 98    2)  96 + _____ = 98    3)  38 + 23 = _____

4)  8 + 92 = _____    5)  3 + _____ = 82    6)  _____ + 73 = 81

7)  45 + 3 = _____    8)  6 + 83 = _____    9)  57 + 7 = _____

10)  51 + 20 = _____    11)  12 + 75 = _____    12)  39 + _____ = 73

13)  21 + _____ = 51    14)  19 + _____ = 63    15)  27 + 21 = _____

16)  56 + _____ = 60    17)  29 + _____ = 64    18)  _____ + 95 = 100

19)  7 + _____ = 38    20)  64 + _____ = 87    21)  _____ + 60 = 97

22)  49 + 41 = _____    23)  66 + 29 = _____    24)  18 + _____ = 64

25)  _____ + 76 = 86    26)  _____ + 83 = 84    27)  30 + _____ = 80

28)  _____ + 34 = 80    29)  12 + _____ = 14    30)  33 + _____ = 49

31)  _____ + 2 = 97    32)  23 + _____ = 55    33)  _____ + 82 = 86

34)  60 + _____ = 92    35)  _____ + 82 = 94    36)  89 + 4 = _____

37)  34 + _____ = 99    38)  2 + 94 = _____    39)  _____ + 20 = 86

40)  12 + 41 = _____    41)  _____ + 1 = 100    42)  _____ + 46 = 56

43)  63 + _____ = 80    44)  52 + 32 = _____    45)  _____ + 77 = 93

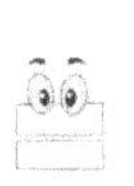

1)  31 + 59 = _____

2)  99 + _____ = 100

3)  _____ + 91 = 94

4)  _____ + 71 = 89

5)  _____ + 30 = 58

6)  _____ + 31 = 91

7)  _____ + 89 = 99

8)  87 + _____ = 96

9)  15 + 60 = _____

10)  _____ + 9 = 21

11)  _____ + 82 = 95

12)  _____ + 92 = 99

13)  10 + 87 = _____

14)  96 + _____ = 99

15)  _____ + 43 = 54

16)  8 + _____ = 85

17)  _____ + 13 = 74

18)  53 + 19 = _____

19)  70 + _____ = 72

20)  _____ + 37 = 62

21)  _____ + 5 = 52

22)  65 + _____ = 72

23)  _____ + 7 = 74

24)  8 + 87 = _____

25)  _____ + 23 = 89

26)  39 + _____ = 62

27)  14 + _____ = 68

28)  _____ + 27 = 85

29)  _____ + 47 = 64

30)  12 + _____ = 64

31)  _____ + 18 = 90

32)  35 + 64 = _____

33)  _____ + 28 = 58

34)  82 + _____ = 95

35)  _____ + 7 = 57

36)  66 + 14 = _____

37)  _____ + 52 = 95

38)  8 + 75 = _____

39)  11 + 69 = _____

40)  46 + 16 = _____

41)  _____ + 26 = 91

42)  _____ + 39 = 78

43)  _____ + 1 = 27

44)  62 + 24 = _____

45)  _____ + 98 = 100

1) $77 + \rule{1cm}{0.15mm} = 99$    2) $\rule{1cm}{0.15mm} + 11 = 14$    3) $\rule{1cm}{0.15mm} + 30 = 45$

4) $63 + \rule{1cm}{0.15mm} = 95$    5) $14 + \rule{1cm}{0.15mm} = 94$    6) $\rule{1cm}{0.15mm} + 32 = 95$

7) $71 + \rule{1cm}{0.15mm} = 73$    8) $60 + 10 = \rule{1cm}{0.15mm}$    9) $8 + \rule{1cm}{0.15mm} = 91$

10) $6 + 86 = \rule{1cm}{0.15mm}$    11) $95 + \rule{1cm}{0.15mm} = 96$    12) $42 + \rule{1cm}{0.15mm} = 69$

13) $5 + \rule{1cm}{0.15mm} = 97$    14) $\rule{1cm}{0.15mm} + 20 = 71$    15) $70 + 26 = \rule{1cm}{0.15mm}$

16) $68 + \rule{1cm}{0.15mm} = 82$    17) $11 + 57 = \rule{1cm}{0.15mm}$    18) $65 + \rule{1cm}{0.15mm} = 85$

19) $\rule{1cm}{0.15mm} + 81 = 95$    20) $31 + \rule{1cm}{0.15mm} = 43$    21) $\rule{1cm}{0.15mm} + 46 = 77$

22) $\rule{1cm}{0.15mm} + 9 = 50$    23) $\rule{1cm}{0.15mm} + 68 = 81$    24) $23 + \rule{1cm}{0.15mm} = 71$

25) $0 + \rule{1cm}{0.15mm} = 92$    26) $80 + \rule{1cm}{0.15mm} = 86$    27) $47 + \rule{1cm}{0.15mm} = 62$

28) $\rule{1cm}{0.15mm} + 82 = 97$    29) $11 + 65 = \rule{1cm}{0.15mm}$    30) $42 + 10 = \rule{1cm}{0.15mm}$

31) $82 + 4 = \rule{1cm}{0.15mm}$    32) $97 + \rule{1cm}{0.15mm} = 99$    33) $\rule{1cm}{0.15mm} + 61 = 65$

34) $17 + \rule{1cm}{0.15mm} = 38$    35) $\rule{1cm}{0.15mm} + 72 = 99$    36) $74 + \rule{1cm}{0.15mm} = 89$

37) $\rule{1cm}{0.15mm} + 15 = 81$    38) $\rule{1cm}{0.15mm} + 100 = 100$    39) $\rule{1cm}{0.15mm} + 5 = 100$

40) $36 + 37 = \rule{1cm}{0.15mm}$    41) $\rule{1cm}{0.15mm} + 35 = 99$    42) $72 + 15 = \rule{1cm}{0.15mm}$

43) $39 + \rule{1cm}{0.15mm} = 53$    44) $\rule{1cm}{0.15mm} + 40 = 92$    45) $42 + \rule{1cm}{0.15mm} = 66$

# MATH

1) _____ + 8 = 87       2) _____ + 62 = 91       3) 25 + _____ = 49

4) _____ + 30 = 79      5) _____ + 35 = 70       6) 8 + _____ = 70

7) 86 + _____ = 90      8) 2 + _____ = 91        9) _____ + 55 = 92

10) 6 + _____ = 78      11) 74 + _____ = 82      12) 51 + _____ = 95

13) 61 + _____ = 85     14) 36 + _____ = 80      15) 50 + _____ = 84

16) 47 + _____ = 49     17) _____ + 4 = 13       18) _____ + 69 = 96

19) 41 + 51 = _____     20) _____ + 22 = 100     21) _____ + 30 = 35

22) 67 + _____ = 89     23) 82 + _____ = 91      24) 74 + _____ = 83

25) 81 + _____ = 92     26) _____ + 23 = 82      27) _____ + 100 = 100

28) 89 + _____ = 93     29) 1 + 72 = _____       30) _____ + 54 = 97

31) 1 + _____ = 90      32) _____ + 14 = 66      33) 20 + 17 = _____

34) 11 + _____ = 76     35) _____ + 15 = 63      36) 17 + 33 = _____

37) 21 + _____ = 87     38) _____ + 49 = 63      39) 82 + 8 = _____

40) _____ + 91 = 96     41) 17 + _____ = 22      42) 53 + _____ = 100

43) _____ + 65 = 72     44) 32 + _____ = 54      45) 32 + _____ = 72

1) 62 + _____ = 83    2) 41 + 34 = _____    3) 44 + _____ = 98

4) _____ + 6 = 38    5) _____ + 6 = 48    6) 19 + 60 = _____

7) 76 + 13 = _____    8) 9 + _____ = 87    9) 96 + _____ = 98

10) 21 + 37 = _____    11) 4 + _____ = 89    12) _____ + 19 = 89

13) 76 + _____ = 83    14) 58 + _____ = 94    15) 7 + 64 = _____

16) _____ + 55 = 97    17) 25 + 68 = _____    18) 4 + _____ = 36

19) _____ + 50 = 91    20) _____ + 39 = 53    21) _____ + 3 = 43

22) 55 + _____ = 96    23) 60 + _____ = 91    24) 18 + _____ = 68

25) 44 + 39 = _____    26) _____ + 15 = 27    27) _____ + 49 = 69

28) 74 + 8 = _____    29) _____ + 41 = 71    30) _____ + 1 = 85

31) _____ + 38 = 56    32) 83 + _____ = 84    33) 21 + 74 = _____

34) _____ + 69 = 79    35) _____ + 19 = 23    36) 56 + _____ = 63

37) _____ + 72 = 98    38) 100 + _____ = 101    39) 21 + _____ = 68

40) 90 + _____ = 93    41) _____ + 25 = 52    42) 48 + _____ = 74

43) 79 + _____ = 94    44) 32 + 3 = _____    45) 13 + _____ = 76

1) 92 + _____ = 96    2) 29 + _____ = 85    3) 38 + _____ = 91

4) 15 + _____ = 91    5) 100 + _____ = 100    6) _____ + 38 = 48

7) _____ + 70 = 84    8) 43 + 34 = _____    9) 5 + _____ = 87

10) 84 + _____ = 93    11) 25 + _____ = 66    12) _____ + 1 = 63

13) 53 + _____ = 90    14) 75 + 2 = _____    15) 46 + _____ = 73

16) 82 + 15 = _____    17) _____ + 13 = 47    18) _____ + 79 = 85

19) 43 + _____ = 65    20) 71 + _____ = 86    21) _____ + 10 = 86

22) _____ + 28 = 95    23) _____ + 25 = 71    24) 83 + _____ = 92

25) _____ + 16 = 55    26) _____ + 97 = 100    27) 7 + 91 = _____

28) 1 + _____ = 18    29) _____ + 24 = 60    30) 9 + 88 = _____

31) 36 + _____ = 95    32) 5 + 62 = _____    33) 97 + _____ = 98

34) 70 + _____ = 79    35) 59 + 28 = _____    36) 6 + _____ = 94

37) _____ + 83 = 97    38) 18 + _____ = 93    39) 15 + _____ = 88

40) _____ + 40 = 83    41) 27 + _____ = 51    42) 1 + 99 = _____

43) 97 + _____ = 100    44) 21 + _____ = 86    45) _____ + 88 = 93

1)  21 + _____ = 100
2)  20 + _____ = 53
3)  _____ + 5 = 71

4)  0 + 100 = _____
5)  _____ + 6 = 45
6)  _____ + 21 = 100

7)  _____ + 28 = 76
8)  5 + _____ = 19
9)  10 + 28 = _____

10)  _____ + 25 = 70
11)  _____ + 62 = 63
12)  _____ + 1 = 82

13)  _____ + 4 = 77
14)  56 + _____ = 70
15)  59 + _____ = 86

16)  _____ + 67 = 95
17)  10 + _____ = 47
18)  25 + _____ = 81

19)  _____ + 75 = 93
20)  _____ + 18 = 49
21)  _____ + 1 = 96

22)  _____ + 3 = 95
23)  98 + _____ = 100
24)  6 + _____ = 97

25)  5 + _____ = 73
26)  89 + 9 = _____
27)  _____ + 44 = 60

28)  _____ + 28 = 67
29)  63 + _____ = 92
30)  16 + _____ = 82

31)  _____ + 19 = 79
32)  19 + 22 = _____
33)  55 + _____ = 57

34)  9 + _____ = 32
35)  _____ + 6 = 57
36)  8 + 74 = _____

37)  29 + _____ = 32
38)  54 + _____ = 67
39)  65 + _____ = 69

40)  _____ + 41 = 57
41)  _____ + 46 = 91
42)  _____ + 0 = 100

43)  41 + 9 = _____
44)  45 + _____ = 54
45)  _____ + 4 = 53

1) 46 + 51 = _____        2) 49 + 48 = _____        3) 17 + 68 = _____

4) _____ + 75 = 79        5) _____ + 66 = 67        6) 55 + _____ = 58

7) _____ + 6 = 64         8) 76 + _____ = 80        9) _____ + 34 = 82

10) 0 + 100 = _____       11) _____ + 58 = 87       12) 34 + 18 = _____

13) 99 + _____ = 100      14) 61 + _____ = 87       15) 59 + _____ = 94

16) 12 + 71 = _____       17) _____ + 4 = 94        18) 92 + _____ = 97

19) _____ + 81 = 85       20) _____ + 71 = 86       21) 68 + 21 = _____

22) _____ + 79 = 98       23) _____ + 20 = 68       24) 42 + _____ = 68

25) 39 + _____ = 47       26) 35 + _____ = 36       27) 5 + _____ = 51

28) 33 + _____ = 98       29) _____ + 15 = 97       30) 15 + _____ = 83

31) 46 + 2 = _____        32) 14 + _____ = 94       33) 86 + 4 = _____

34) 10 + _____ = 100      35) _____ + 17 = 28       36) _____ + 6 = 90

37) 89 + 2 = _____        38) _____ + 56 = 81       39) _____ + 42 = 46

40) 5 + _____ = 57        41) _____ + 13 = 99       42) 73 + _____ = 82

43) 40 + 23 = _____       44) 89 + 1 = _____        45) _____ + 16 = 81

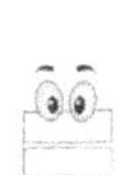

# Subtraction
# 0-50

1) 19 − 9 = _____    2) 9 − 2 = _____    3) 2 − 1 = _____

4) 40 − 30 = _____    5) 34 − 6 = _____    6) 21 − 6 = _____

7) 45 − 33 = _____    8) 24 − 14 = _____    9) 17 − 1 = _____

10) 25 − 21 = _____    11) 5 − 3 = _____    12) 47 − 36 = _____

13) 18 − 12 = _____    14) 49 − 33 = _____    15) 33 − 14 = _____

16) 10 − 8 = _____    17) 32 − 29 = _____    18) 48 − 34 = _____

19) 40 − 3 = _____    20) 18 − 10 = _____    21) 20 − 3 = _____

22) 24 − 20 = _____    23) 35 − 23 = _____    24) 19 − 9 = _____

25) 24 − 21 = _____    26) 27 − 24 = _____    27) 16 − 13 = _____

28) 47 − 6 = _____    29) 43 − 28 = _____    30) 9 − 8 = _____

31) 28 − 15 = _____    32) 36 − 18 = _____    33) 33 − 32 = _____

34) 47 − 24 = _____    35) 38 − 12 = _____    36) 40 − 36 = _____

37) 12 − 7 = _____    38) 44 − 20 = _____    39) 30 − 9 = _____

40) 38 − 25 = _____    41) 22 − 12 = _____    42) 49 − 24 = _____

43) 47 − 20 = _____    44) 44 − 22 = _____    45) 31 − 12 = _____

1) 38 − 20 = _____  2) 27 − 1 = _____  3) 40 − 7 = _____

4) 23 − 4 = _____  5) 38 − 35 = _____  6) 38 − 3 = _____

7) 38 − 27 = _____  8) 15 − 8 = _____  9) 41 − 11 = _____

10) 40 − 24 = _____  11) 46 − 3 = _____  12) 44 − 1 = _____

13) 9 − 8 = _____  14) 13 − 7 = _____  15) 28 − 17 = _____

16) 8 − 6 = _____  17) 20 − 4 = _____  18) 49 − 11 = _____

19) 26 − 3 = _____  20) 44 − 2 = _____  21) 39 − 30 = _____

22) 41 − 12 = _____  23) 44 − 19 = _____  24) 37 − 9 = _____

25) 33 − 12 = _____  26) 16 − 12 = _____  27) 47 − 36 = _____

28) 41 − 15 = _____  29) 44 − 16 = _____  30) 43 − 40 = _____

31) 50 − 14 = _____  32) 49 − 16 = _____  33) 6 − 5 = _____

34) 45 − 45 = _____  35) 27 − 0 = _____  36) 45 − 13 = _____

37) 49 − 36 = _____  38) 10 − 1 = _____  39) 45 − 34 = _____

40) 42 − 25 = _____  41) 48 − 37 = _____  42) 45 − 44 = _____

43) 6 − 4 = _____  44) 33 − 7 = _____  45) 27 − 23 = _____

1)  42 − 39 = _____    2)  43 − 38 = _____    3)  40 − 25 = _____

4)  21 − 10 = _____    5)  48 − 6 = _____    6)  49 − 18 = _____

7)  48 − 2 = _____    8)  8 − 0 = _____    9)  38 − 31 = _____

10)  38 − 16 = _____    11)  46 − 15 = _____    12)  25 − 20 = _____

13)  25 − 21 = _____    14)  30 − 10 = _____    15)  32 − 5 = _____

16)  28 − 27 = _____    17)  40 − 36 = _____    18)  32 − 28 = _____

19)  42 − 3 = _____    20)  25 − 20 = _____    21)  49 − 25 = _____

22)  49 − 3 = _____    23)  20 − 5 = _____    24)  19 − 14 = _____

25)  4 − 4 = _____    26)  28 − 0 = _____    27)  6 − 0 = _____

28)  29 − 18 = _____    29)  39 − 31 = _____    30)  17 − 13 = _____

31)  36 − 26 = _____    32)  37 − 1 = _____    33)  44 − 40 = _____

34)  36 − 2 = _____    35)  36 − 16 = _____    36)  27 − 0 = _____

37)  26 − 24 = _____    38)  28 − 1 = _____    39)  28 − 22 = _____

40)  41 − 6 = _____    41)  34 − 16 = _____    42)  9 − 0 = _____

43)  41 − 30 = _____    44)  42 − 15 = _____    45)  43 − 9 = _____

1) 21 − 17 = _____    2) 28 − 22 = _____    3) 27 − 13 = _____

4) 34 − 30 = _____    5) 47 − 34 = _____    6) 17 − 4 = _____

7) 36 − 22 = _____    8) 47 − 11 = _____    9) 24 − 11 = _____

10) 16 − 13 = _____    11) 22 − 0 = _____    12) 42 − 28 = _____

13) 46 − 16 = _____    14) 29 − 1 = _____    15) 39 − 23 = _____

16) 50 − 42 = _____    17) 17 − 6 = _____    18) 32 − 22 = _____

19) 47 − 5 = _____    20) 31 − 7 = _____    21) 47 − 38 = _____

22) 30 − 1 = _____    23) 33 − 32 = _____    24) 22 − 4 = _____

25) 40 − 17 = _____    26) 14 − 12 = _____    27) 39 − 14 = _____

28) 41 − 2 = _____    29) 21 − 13 = _____    30) 28 − 12 = _____

31) 25 − 20 = _____    32) 26 − 20 = _____    33) 45 − 44 = _____

34) 27 − 16 = _____    35) 50 − 28 = _____    36) 23 − 22 = _____

37) 41 − 23 = _____    38) 39 − 19 = _____    39) 23 − 2 = _____

40) 23 − 4 = _____    41) 41 − 19 = _____    42) 6 − 3 = _____

43) 7 − 6 = _____    44) 48 − 2 = _____    45) 20 − 3 = _____

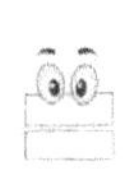

1) 32 – 22 = _____    2) 20 – 15 = _____    3) 31 – 6 = _____

4) 39 – 29 = _____    5) 48 – 19 = _____    6) 41 – 9 = _____

7) 25 – 2 = _____    8) 43 – 23 = _____    9) 12 – 7 = _____

10) 19 – 11 = _____    11) 16 – 1 = _____    12) 1 – 1 = _____

13) 21 – 16 = _____    14) 49 – 2 = _____    15) 33 – 32 = _____

16) 41 – 29 = _____    17) 50 – 41 = _____    18) 50 – 12 = _____

19) 47 – 41 = _____    20) 50 – 34 = _____    21) 45 – 43 = _____

22) 35 – 29 = _____    23) 47 – 27 = _____    24) 31 – 5 = _____

25) 14 – 10 = _____    26) 42 – 39 = _____    27) 38 – 27 = _____

28) 20 – 20 = _____    29) 15 – 1 = _____    30) 44 – 36 = _____

31) 24 – 16 = _____    32) 16 – 5 = _____    33) 39 – 34 = _____

34) 41 – 11 = _____    35) 41 – 15 = _____    36) 25 – 11 = _____

37) 39 – 3 = _____    38) 32 – 5 = _____    39) 31 – 13 = _____

40) 4 – 2 = _____    41) 47 – 33 = _____    42) 49 – 27 = _____

43) 30 – 24 = _____    44) 39 – 27 = _____    45) 43 – 21 = _____

1)  38 – 32 = _____    2)  43 – 43 = _____    3)  32 – 8 = _____

4)  50 – 34 = _____    5)  31 – 9 = _____    6)  5 – 4 = _____

7)  50 – 7 = _____    8)  35 – 6 = _____    9)  37 – 9 = _____

10)  47 – 40 = _____    11)  47 – 26 = _____    12)  35 – 24 = _____

13)  16 – 11 = _____    14)  39 – 15 = _____    15)  31 – 26 = _____

16)  20 – 11 = _____    17)  45 – 37 = _____    18)  47 – 11 = _____

19)  9 – 7 = _____    20)  12 – 6 = _____    21)  25 – 4 = _____

22)  49 – 20 = _____    23)  40 – 19 = _____    24)  25 – 20 = _____

25)  34 – 2 = _____    26)  32 – 7 = _____    27)  18 – 10 = _____

28)  34 – 23 = _____    29)  29 – 19 = _____    30)  23 – 13 = _____

31)  38 – 8 = _____    32)  39 – 10 = _____    33)  46 – 31 = _____

34)  15 – 3 = _____    35)  43 – 37 = _____    36)  46 – 29 = _____

37)  26 – 17 = _____    38)  36 – 34 = _____    39)  44 – 2 = _____

40)  49 – 35 = _____    41)  37 – 0 = _____    42)  20 – 4 = _____

43)  30 – 1 = _____    44)  30 – 23 = _____    45)  24 – 1 = _____

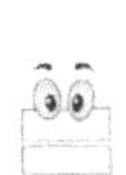

1)  43 − 2 = _____    2)  32 − 18 = _____    3)  7 − 3 = _____

4)  46 − 19 = _____    5)  39 − 17 = _____    6)  19 − 6 = _____

7)  38 − 22 = _____    8)  45 − 12 = _____    9)  16 − 6 = _____

10)  27 − 25 = _____    11)  37 − 36 = _____    12)  47 − 11 = _____

13)  38 − 1 = _____    14)  40 − 13 = _____    15)  47 − 33 = _____

16)  32 − 11 = _____    17)  46 − 22 = _____    18)  29 − 4 = _____

19)  19 − 5 = _____    20)  50 − 24 = _____    21)  17 − 3 = _____

22)  19 − 10 = _____    23)  37 − 15 = _____    24)  42 − 11 = _____

25)  41 − 37 = _____    26)  44 − 19 = _____    27)  30 − 19 = _____

28)  31 − 18 = _____    29)  41 − 21 = _____    30)  48 − 45 = _____

31)  21 − 14 = _____    32)  32 − 28 = _____    33)  41 − 20 = _____

34)  41 − 3 = _____    35)  29 − 1 = _____    36)  9 − 2 = _____

37)  24 − 8 = _____    38)  29 − 6 = _____    39)  41 − 25 = _____

40)  26 − 15 = _____    41)  42 − 14 = _____    42)  41 − 24 = _____

43)  46 − 23 = _____    44)  12 − 2 = _____    45)  38 − 3 = _____

1) 29 – 18 = _____     2) 45 – 31 = _____     3) 30 – 2 = _____

4) 35 – 9 = _____     5) 40 – 24 = _____     6) 32 – 15 = _____

7) 40 – 29 = _____     8) 32 – 5 = _____     9) 48 – 6 = _____

10) 44 – 5 = _____     11) 32 – 16 = _____     12) 28 – 24 = _____

13) 43 – 14 = _____     14) 3 – 1 = _____     15) 36 – 19 = _____

16) 37 – 23 = _____     17) 40 – 13 = _____     18) 33 – 19 = _____

19) 40 – 17 = _____     20) 20 – 14 = _____     21) 9 – 5 = _____

22) 40 – 19 = _____     23) 43 – 19 = _____     24) 50 – 42 = _____

25) 49 – 8 = _____     26) 46 – 33 = _____     27) 4 – 2 = _____

28) 44 – 43 = _____     29) 19 – 16 = _____     30) 30 – 12 = _____

31) 45 – 38 = _____     32) 42 – 40 = _____     33) 36 – 11 = _____

34) 34 – 11 = _____     35) 47 – 44 = _____     36) 34 – 15 = _____

37) 45 – 14 = _____     38) 38 – 19 = _____     39) 13 – 13 = _____

40) 17 – 12 = _____     41) 37 – 1 = _____     42) 24 – 17 = _____

43) 50 – 25 = _____     44) 35 – 30 = _____     45) 35 – 19 = _____

1) $24 - 2 =$ _____    2) $35 - 33 =$ _____    3) $49 - 30 =$ _____

4) $46 - 42 =$ _____    5) $49 - 23 =$ _____    6) $50 - 5 =$ _____

7) $21 - 16 =$ _____    8) $43 - 27 =$ _____    9) $31 - 0 =$ _____

10) $11 - 7 =$ _____    11) $30 - 6 =$ _____    12) $9 - 6 =$ _____

13) $35 - 34 =$ _____    14) $44 - 15 =$ _____    15) $50 - 34 =$ _____

16) $37 - 26 =$ _____    17) $39 - 14 =$ _____    18) $28 - 10 =$ _____

19) $32 - 5 =$ _____    20) $29 - 18 =$ _____    21) $42 - 35 =$ _____

22) $41 - 20 =$ _____    23) $36 - 11 =$ _____    24) $49 - 42 =$ _____

25) $17 - 4 =$ _____    26) $43 - 15 =$ _____    27) $19 - 11 =$ _____

28) $49 - 37 =$ _____    29) $46 - 9 =$ _____    30) $49 - 42 =$ _____

31) $35 - 12 =$ _____    32) $16 - 15 =$ _____    33) $6 - 4 =$ _____

34) $38 - 25 =$ _____    35) $24 - 17 =$ _____    36) $11 - 5 =$ _____

37) $13 - 9 =$ _____    38) $35 - 19 =$ _____    39) $27 - 5 =$ _____

40) $48 - 27 =$ _____    41) $43 - 28 =$ _____    42) $40 - 33 =$ _____

43) $39 - 21 =$ _____    44) $22 - 7 =$ _____    45) $41 - 0 =$ _____

1) 36 − 28 = _____    2) 36 − 18 = _____    3) 48 − 40 = _____

4) 46 − 4 = _____    5) 31 − 18 = _____    6) 42 − 31 = _____

7) 36 − 7 = _____    8) 42 − 37 = _____    9) 48 − 17 = _____

10) 45 − 38 = _____    11) 7 − 1 = _____    12) 44 − 42 = _____

13) 49 − 36 = _____    14) 47 − 13 = _____    15) 49 − 25 = _____

16) 33 − 8 = _____    17) 9 − 3 = _____    18) 16 − 4 = _____

19) 45 − 38 = _____    20) 48 − 38 = _____    21) 30 − 16 = _____

22) 30 − 5 = _____    23) 28 − 24 = _____    24) 33 − 11 = _____

25) 35 − 25 = _____    26) 18 − 12 = _____    27) 31 − 25 = _____

28) 14 − 3 = _____    29) 10 − 0 = _____    30) 41 − 18 = _____

31) 19 − 2 = _____    32) 23 − 12 = _____    33) 36 − 20 = _____

34) 15 − 13 = _____    35) 27 − 27 = _____    36) 32 − 2 = _____

37) 46 − 34 = _____    38) 48 − 31 = _____    39) 48 − 46 = _____

40) 29 − 4 = _____    41) 21 − 5 = _____    42) 31 − 11 = _____

43) 38 − 28 = _____    44) 37 − 27 = _____    45) 13 − 7 = _____

# Subtraction
# 0-100

1) 100 − 62 = _____    2) 40 − 19 = _____    3) 79 − 5 = _____

4) 73 − 23 = _____    5) 52 − 16 = _____    6) 71 − 71 = _____

7) 43 − 13 = _____    8) 74 − 53 = _____    9) 99 − 52 = _____

10) 78 − 65 = _____    11) 91 − 77 = _____    12) 81 − 21 = _____

13) 1 − 1 = _____    14) 46 − 33 = _____    15) 67 − 8 = _____

16) 99 − 39 = _____    17) 93 − 54 = _____    18) 70 − 57 = _____

19) 45 − 27 = _____    20) 26 − 2 = _____    21) 61 − 3 = _____

22) 85 − 15 = _____    23) 53 − 17 = _____    24) 79 − 57 = _____

25) 58 − 13 = _____    26) 84 − 23 = _____    27) 86 − 4 = _____

28) 48 − 45 = _____    29) 19 − 7 = _____    30) 26 − 25 = _____

31) 87 − 68 = _____    32) 8 − 7 = _____    33) 26 − 26 = _____

34) 83 − 63 = _____    35) 45 − 29 = _____    36) 79 − 47 = _____

37) 73 − 64 = _____    38) 18 − 11 = _____    39) 90 − 70 = _____

40) 82 − 42 = _____    41) 51 − 12 = _____    42) 78 − 12 = _____

43) 89 − 61 = _____    44) 97 − 83 = _____    45) 97 − 13 = _____

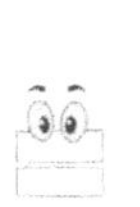

# MATH

1) 52 – 46 = _____      2) 60 – 34 = _____      3) 83 – 29 = _____

4) 92 – 10 = _____      5) 94 – 69 = _____      6) 36 – 6 = _____

7) 57 – 54 = _____      8) 64 – 42 = _____      9) 69 – 2 = _____

10) 80 – 13 = _____     11) 57 – 2 = _____      12) 92 – 73 = _____

13) 39 – 8 = _____      14) 93 – 42 = _____     15) 95 – 94 = _____

16) 8 – 1 = _____       17) 23 – 22 = _____     18) 33 – 11 = _____

19) 90 – 14 = _____     20) 86 – 16 = _____     21) 52 – 42 = _____

22) 32 – 31 = _____     23) 100 – 66 = _____    24) 57 – 37 = _____

25) 42 – 6 = _____      26) 93 – 51 = _____     27) 95 – 18 = _____

28) 80 – 71 = _____     29) 32 – 9 = _____      30) 82 – 50 = _____

31) 98 – 94 = _____     32) 78 – 14 = _____     33) 62 – 60 = _____

34) 30 – 25 = _____     35) 59 – 12 = _____     36) 34 – 25 = _____

37) 99 – 79 = _____     38) 19 – 9 = _____      39) 74 – 13 = _____

40) 63 – 27 = _____     41) 63 – 20 = _____     42) 91 – 27 = _____

43) 73 – 20 = _____     44) 66 – 52 = _____     45) 31 – 2 = _____

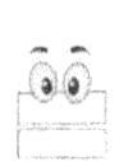

1) 69 – 32 = _____   2) 95 – 68 = _____   3) 55 – 9 = _____

4) 98 – 33 = _____   5) 62 – 34 = _____   6) 76 – 62 = _____

7) 95 – 7 = _____   8) 56 – 20 = _____   9) 19 – 17 = _____

10) 97 – 19 = _____   11) 72 – 68 = _____   12) 40 – 38 = _____

13) 47 – 10 = _____   14) 45 – 43 = _____   15) 37 – 37 = _____

16) 95 – 94 = _____   17) 70 – 17 = _____   18) 87 – 35 = _____

19) 80 – 39 = _____   20) 66 – 18 = _____   21) 98 – 7 = _____

22) 38 – 26 = _____   23) 91 – 53 = _____   24) 82 – 63 = _____

25) 63 – 42 = _____   26) 37 – 19 = _____   27) 27 – 24 = _____

28) 99 – 5 = _____   29) 11 – 10 = _____   30) 74 – 70 = _____

31) 92 – 12 = _____   32) 85 – 22 = _____   33) 90 – 69 = _____

34) 49 – 43 = _____   35) 86 – 25 = _____   36) 41 – 28 = _____

37) 48 – 39 = _____   38) 34 – 33 = _____   39) 61 – 44 = _____

40) 54 – 12 = _____   41) 85 – 61 = _____   42) 43 – 20 = _____

43) 92 – 42 = _____   44) 69 – 21 = _____   45) 67 – 20 = _____

# MATH

1) $100 - 71 =$ _____    2) $77 - 14 =$ _____    3) $83 - 39 =$ _____

4) $86 - 78 =$ _____    5) $96 - 39 =$ _____    6) $85 - 60 =$ _____

7) $46 - 23 =$ _____    8) $65 - 46 =$ _____    9) $99 - 42 =$ _____

10) $90 - 67 =$ _____    11) $58 - 29 =$ _____    12) $65 - 8 =$ _____

13) $91 - 81 =$ _____    14) $68 - 61 =$ _____    15) $66 - 45 =$ _____

16) $11 - 5 =$ _____    17) $75 - 50 =$ _____    18) $71 - 41 =$ _____

19) $96 - 28 =$ _____    20) $90 - 56 =$ _____    21) $35 - 27 =$ _____

22) $95 - 41 =$ _____    23) $95 - 36 =$ _____    24) $60 - 7 =$ _____

25) $56 - 22 =$ _____    26) $67 - 35 =$ _____    27) $75 - 3 =$ _____

28) $75 - 50 =$ _____    29) $78 - 45 =$ _____    30) $52 - 6 =$ _____

31) $29 - 12 =$ _____    32) $79 - 38 =$ _____    33) $56 - 31 =$ _____

34) $79 - 46 =$ _____    35) $90 - 3 =$ _____    36) $88 - 27 =$ _____

37) $65 - 36 =$ _____    38) $74 - 44 =$ _____    39) $37 - 33 =$ _____

40) $85 - 72 =$ _____    41) $73 - 12 =$ _____    42) $98 - 7 =$ _____

43) $42 - 35 =$ _____    44) $32 - 12 =$ _____    45) $88 - 15 =$ _____

1) 94 − 65 = _____        2) 32 − 10 = _____        3) 48 − 23 = _____

4) 97 − 49 = _____        5) 86 − 3 = _____        6) 67 − 15 = _____

7) 95 − 58 = _____        8) 66 − 48 = _____        9) 59 − 28 = _____

10) 88 − 37 = _____        11) 40 − 19 = _____        12) 8 − 1 = _____

13) 97 − 2 = _____        14) 91 − 68 = _____        15) 32 − 31 = _____

16) 94 − 84 = _____        17) 92 − 60 = _____        18) 47 − 31 = _____

19) 27 − 21 = _____        20) 94 − 10 = _____        21) 69 − 56 = _____

22) 34 − 28 = _____        23) 83 − 71 = _____        24) 60 − 56 = _____

25) 68 − 26 = _____        26) 92 − 49 = _____        27) 58 − 44 = _____

28) 100 − 35 = _____        29) 56 − 39 = _____        30) 61 − 53 = _____

31) 95 − 2 = _____        32) 77 − 59 = _____        33) 60 − 49 = _____

34) 67 − 61 = _____        35) 92 − 32 = _____        36) 87 − 73 = _____

37) 68 − 59 = _____        38) 72 − 17 = _____        39) 99 − 28 = _____

40) 82 − 58 = _____        41) 72 − 60 = _____        42) 80 − 20 = _____

43) 97 − 67 = _____        44) 92 − 13 = _____        45) 67 − 47 = _____

1) 80 – 71 = _____     2) 89 – 46 = _____     3) 28 – 2 = _____

4) 98 – 81 = _____     5) 51 – 50 = _____     6) 50 – 47 = _____

7) 73 – 71 = _____     8) 32 – 11 = _____     9) 65 – 51 = _____

10) 72 – 15 = _____     11) 20 – 11 = _____     12) 93 – 80 = _____

13) 99 – 27 = _____     14) 77 – 70 = _____     15) 18 – 14 = _____

16) 99 – 64 = _____     17) 93 – 61 = _____     18) 96 – 62 = _____

19) 61 – 44 = _____     20) 63 – 48 = _____     21) 41 – 7 = _____

22) 30 – 16 = _____     23) 89 – 53 = _____     24) 48 – 40 = _____

25) 98 – 49 = _____     26) 93 – 41 = _____     27) 40 – 12 = _____

28) 58 – 36 = _____     29) 74 – 67 = _____     30) 80 – 33 = _____

31) 35 – 23 = _____     32) 27 – 16 = _____     33) 62 – 47 = _____

34) 100 – 86 = _____     35) 73 – 47 = _____     36) 75 – 75 = _____

37) 69 – 58 = _____     38) 84 – 60 = _____     39) 90 – 37 = _____

40) 98 – 9 = _____     41) 87 – 11 = _____     42) 62 – 48 = _____

43) 22 – 19 = _____     44) 73 – 61 = _____     45) 51 – 16 = _____

1)  95 – 94 = _____      2)  43 – 38 = _____      3)  43 – 11 = _____

4)  76 – 66 = _____      5)  100 – 14 = _____      6)  67 – 10 = _____

7)  64 – 41 = _____      8)  74 – 1 = _____      9)  8 – 2 = _____

10)  78 – 28 = _____      11)  91 – 76 = _____      12)  48 – 17 = _____

13)  59 – 17 = _____      14)  72 – 24 = _____      15)  91 – 71 = _____

16)  43 – 11 = _____      17)  65 – 16 = _____      18)  79 – 20 = _____

19)  87 – 32 = _____      20)  99 – 76 = _____      21)  63 – 46 = _____

22)  91 – 74 = _____      23)  76 – 70 = _____      24)  64 – 20 = _____

25)  12 – 5 = _____      26)  79 – 31 = _____      27)  52 – 1 = _____

28)  96 – 72 = _____      29)  90 – 34 = _____      30)  33 – 10 = _____

31)  61 – 34 = _____      32)  76 – 60 = _____      33)  53 – 23 = _____

34)  86 – 57 = _____      35)  58 – 43 = _____      36)  31 – 30 = _____

37)  100 – 61 = _____      38)  63 – 50 = _____      39)  88 – 66 = _____

40)  78 – 39 = _____      41)  63 – 59 = _____      42)  47 – 31 = _____

43)  94 – 6 = _____      44)  62 – 46 = _____      45)  60 – 27 = _____

1)  70 − 56 = _____    2)  54 − 14 = _____    3)  82 − 40 = _____

4)  30 − 24 = _____    5)  77 − 38 = _____    6)  81 − 9 = _____

7)  83 − 51 = _____    8)  99 − 65 = _____    9)  79 − 70 = _____

10)  48 − 14 = _____    11)  63 − 42 = _____    12)  88 − 18 = _____

13)  89 − 10 = _____    14)  55 − 17 = _____    15)  37 − 18 = _____

16)  93 − 27 = _____    17)  60 − 8 = _____    18)  63 − 14 = _____

19)  97 − 15 = _____    20)  77 − 68 = _____    21)  76 − 30 = _____

22)  42 − 28 = _____    23)  95 − 29 = _____    24)  82 − 38 = _____

25)  54 − 19 = _____    26)  74 − 53 = _____    27)  95 − 44 = _____

28)  80 − 76 = _____    29)  65 − 9 = _____    30)  78 − 55 = _____

31)  48 − 9 = _____    32)  72 − 15 = _____    33)  85 − 43 = _____

34)  65 − 63 = _____    35)  59 − 16 = _____    36)  92 − 91 = _____

37)  10 − 4 = _____    38)  80 − 23 = _____    39)  42 − 24 = _____

40)  37 − 9 = _____    41)  87 − 41 = _____    42)  58 − 33 = _____

43)  18 − 15 = _____    44)  83 − 18 = _____    45)  96 − 79 = _____

1) 27 − 16 = _____      2) 52 − 29 = _____      3) 69 − 28 = _____

4) 91 − 57 = _____      5) 22 − 13 = _____      6) 52 − 26 = _____

7) 85 − 23 = _____      8) 92 − 49 = _____      9) 25 − 1 = _____

10) 67 − 34 = _____     11) 35 − 7 = _____      12) 56 − 52 = _____

13) 35 − 11 = _____     14) 74 − 33 = _____     15) 94 − 58 = _____

16) 57 − 4 = _____      17) 91 − 79 = _____     18) 82 − 15 = _____

19) 47 − 6 = _____      20) 71 − 30 = _____     21) 74 − 35 = _____

22) 92 − 30 = _____     23) 91 − 25 = _____     24) 88 − 19 = _____

25) 19 − 1 = _____      26) 92 − 33 = _____     27) 87 − 52 = _____

28) 79 − 11 = _____     29) 65 − 7 = _____      30) 89 − 6 = _____

31) 61 − 52 = _____     32) 25 − 8 = _____      33) 99 − 53 = _____

34) 12 − 3 = _____      35) 77 − 51 = _____     36) 81 − 12 = _____

37) 38 − 27 = _____     38) 86 − 43 = _____     39) 34 − 22 = _____

40) 30 − 8 = _____      41) 86 − 48 = _____     42) 55 − 37 = _____

43) 94 − 66 = _____     44) 64 − 32 = _____     45) 84 − 74 = _____

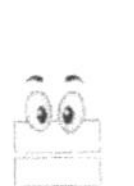

1) 91 − 82 = _____     2) 92 − 33 = _____     3) 35 − 0 = _____

4) 94 − 74 = _____     5) 73 − 72 = _____     6) 79 − 15 = _____

7) 92 − 59 = _____     8) 64 − 59 = _____     9) 22 − 14 = _____

10) 97 − 18 = _____    11) 42 − 34 = _____    12) 29 − 26 = _____

13) 97 − 17 = _____    14) 74 − 70 = _____    15) 72 − 61 = _____

16) 55 − 17 = _____    17) 99 − 25 = _____    18) 25 − 18 = _____

19) 64 − 64 = _____    20) 63 − 28 = _____    21) 36 − 11 = _____

22) 61 − 31 = _____    23) 76 − 71 = _____    24) 48 − 42 = _____

25) 55 − 43 = _____    26) 50 − 26 = _____    27) 28 − 20 = _____

28) 78 − 4 = _____     29) 49 − 22 = _____    30) 97 − 25 = _____

31) 91 − 38 = _____    32) 46 − 41 = _____    33) 50 − 38 = _____

34) 80 − 79 = _____    35) 64 − 41 = _____    36) 69 − 67 = _____

37) 33 − 29 = _____    38) 70 − 8 = _____     39) 56 − 11 = _____

40) 16 − 4 = _____     41) 74 − 16 = _____    42) 96 − 41 = _____

43) 99 − 56 = _____    44) 72 − 21 = _____    45) 54 − 14 = _____

 **MATH**

# Missing Number
# 0-50

1)  33 − ____ = 26          2)  28 − ____ = 16          3)  ____ − 22 = 19

4)  26 − ____ = 14          5)  47 − ____ = 4           6)  40 − 16 = ____

7)  ____ − 14 = 5           8)  12 − ____ = 9           9)  39 − ____ = 1

10)  48 − ____ = 30         11)  27 − 24 = ____         12)  43 − ____ = 35

13)  ____ − 24 = 14         14)  ____ − 32 = 1          15)  25 − ____ = 6

16)  11 − ____ = 9          17)  7 − 4 = ____           18)  49 − 8 = ____

19)  ____ − 13 = 24         20)  45 − ____ = 13         21)  ____ − 28 = 18

22)  36 − ____ = 10         23)  40 − 21 = ____         24)  30 − ____ = 8

25)  39 − ____ = 4          26)  27 − ____ = 18         27)  25 − ____ = 24

28)  ____ − 11 = 3          29)  31 − 1 = ____          30)  ____ − 4 = 41

31)  49 − ____ = 29         32)  16 − ____ = 7          33)  46 − ____ = 30

34)  40 − ____ = 39         35)  ____ − 28 = 8          36)  50 − 40 = ____

37)  ____ − 21 = 17         38)  45 − 42 = ____         39)  ____ − 11 = 23

40)  21 − ____ = 4          41)  ____ − 3 = 39          42)  31 − 15 = ____

43)  23 − ____ = 3          44)  ____ − 10 = 5          45)  ____ − 7 = 5

  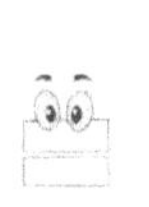

1) _____ − 28 = 1

2) _____ − 22 = 25

3) 35 − _____ = 35

4) _____ − 13 = 2

5) 20 − 8 = _____

6) 44 − 39 = _____

7) _____ − 9 = 27

8) 7 − _____ = 5

9) 32 − _____ = 27

10) 42 − _____ = 18

11) _____ − 14 = 1

12) 36 − _____ = 30

13) 43 − _____ = 25

14) _____ − 33 = 13

15) 45 − _____ = 19

16) 48 − 14 = _____

17) _____ − 7 = 36

18) _____ − 18 = 23

19) 26 − _____ = 17

20) _____ − 2 = 6

21) 3 − _____ = 1

22) 39 − 35 = _____

23) _____ − 15 = 35

24) 40 − _____ = 15

25) 12 − 11 = _____

26) 23 − _____ = 15

27) 25 − 23 = _____

28) _____ − 23 = 16

29) 46 − _____ = 14

30) _____ − 26 = 14

31) 41 − _____ = 24

32) 32 − 29 = _____

33) 49 − _____ = 35

34) 33 − 1 = _____

35) _____ − 1 = 7

36) _____ − 39 = 6

37) _____ − 7 = 31

38) _____ − 0 = 25

39) _____ − 6 = 8

40) _____ − 6 = 25

41) _____ − 1 = 39

42) _____ − 14 = 36

43) 49 − _____ = 19

44) 49 − 18 = _____

45) _____ − 21 = 20

1) _____ − 36 = 4       2) 40 − _____ = 36       3) 16 − _____ = 12

4) 26 − _____ = 0       5) _____ − 16 = 10       6) 49 − _____ = 31

7) 40 − _____ = 18      8) 40 − _____ = 25       9) 43 − _____ = 24

10) 31 − _____ = 29     11) 43 − 20 = _____      12) 22 − _____ = 11

13) _____ − 7 = 21      14) 39 − _____ = 3       15) _____ − 4 = 36

16) 23 − _____ = 0      17) 47 − _____ = 38      18) 45 − _____ = 37

19) 48 − _____ = 18     20) 23 − 10 = _____      21) 23 − 2 = _____

22) 28 − 10 = _____     23) 39 − _____ = 22      24) 33 − _____ = 21

25) _____ − 29 = 17     26) _____ − 5 = 36       27) 41 − _____ = 18

28) 36 − _____ = 33     29) 37 − 17 = _____      30) _____ − 16 = 32

31) _____ − 10 = 34     32) _____ − 4 = 13       33) _____ − 10 = 36

34) 48 − _____ = 41     35) 32 − _____ = 20      36) 48 − 19 = _____

37) 29 − _____ = 4      38) 45 − _____ = 1       39) 11 − _____ = 10

40) 22 − _____ = 20     41) 35 − _____ = 27      42) 31 − _____ = 18

43) 11 − 10 = _____     44) 5 − _____ = 3        45) 35 − 28 = _____

1) _____ − 25 = 21     2) 45 − _____ = 44     3) 24 − 13 = _____

4) 40 − 15 = _____     5) _____ − 3 = 37     6) _____ − 16 = 23

7) 25 − _____ = 12     8) 43 − _____ = 9     9) _____ − 9 = 14

10) _____ − 12 = 10     11) _____ − 10 = 13     12) 11 − 9 = _____

13) 25 − _____ = 17     14) _____ − 2 = 39     15) _____ − 15 = 5

16) 43 − _____ = 32     17) 49 − 42 = _____     18) 38 − _____ = 25

19) _____ − 4 = 10     20) 46 − _____ = 15     21) _____ − 30 = 8

22) _____ − 5 = 42     23) 46 − _____ = 23     24) 28 − _____ = 2

25) _____ − 11 = 17     26) 39 − _____ = 33     27) 27 − _____ = 18

28) 43 − 37 = _____     29) 31 − _____ = 15     30) 43 − 1 = _____

31) 38 − 27 = _____     32) _____ − 6 = 19     33) 30 − _____ = 19

34) 27 − 5 = _____     35) _____ − 21 = 26     36) _____ − 33 = 11

37) 39 − 25 = _____     38) 32 − _____ = 29     39) 40 − _____ = 19

40) 18 − _____ = 1     41) _____ − 5 = 33     42) 29 − 21 = _____

43) _____ − 13 = 34     44) _____ − 2 = 4     45) 41 − 33 = _____

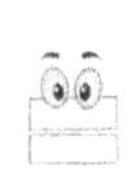

1) 34 − 4 = _____     2) 46 − _____ = 24     3) 28 − _____ = 18

4) 49 − _____ = 35     5) _____ − 3 = 44     6) 12 − _____ = 1

7) _____ − 17 = 33     8) _____ − 43 = 0     9) 39 − _____ = 32

10) _____ − 18 = 24     11) 7 − 3 = _____     12) 48 − _____ = 16

13) _____ − 46 = 1     14) 45 − _____ = 44     15) 30 − _____ = 0

16) 11 − 4 = _____     17) 47 − _____ = 46     18) 19 − _____ = 18

19) _____ − 9 = 22     20) 23 − _____ = 9     21) 27 − _____ = 12

22) 23 − _____ = 18     23) _____ − 16 = 8     24) 26 − _____ = 20

25) 15 − _____ = 2     26) _____ − 18 = 31     27) _____ − 1 = 36

28) 50 − _____ = 2     29) 17 − _____ = 4     30) 20 − _____ = 11

31) 25 − _____ = 21     32) 31 − 7 = _____     33) 30 − 6 = _____

34) 19 − 15 = _____     35) 13 − _____ = 7     36) _____ − 7 = 27

37) _____ − 1 = 17     38) 8 − _____ = 4     39) 32 − _____ = 7

40) _____ − 26 = 1     41) 22 − 8 = _____     42) 31 − 3 = _____

43) 40 − 15 = _____     44) _____ − 17 = 1     45) 28 − _____ = 20

1) 49 – _____ = 17    2) 36 – _____ = 15    3) _____ – 34 = 9

4) _____ – 31 = 4    5) _____ – 42 = 5    6) 22 – _____ = 21

7) 15 – _____ = 4    8) 20 – _____ = 10    9) 47 – _____ = 10

10) 26 – _____ = 14    11) _____ – 22 = 5    12) _____ – 27 = 21

13) 33 – _____ = 1    14) 19 – _____ = 4    15) 44 – _____ = 4

16) _____ – 15 = 12    17) _____ – 37 = 10    18) _____ – 6 = 34

19) 21 – 8 = _____    20) 44 – _____ = 36    21) 37 – _____ = 33

22) 28 – _____ = 23    23) _____ – 23 = 24    24) _____ – 24 = 10

25) 26 – _____ = 14    26) 36 – 1 = _____    27) _____ – 15 = 29

28) 47 – 16 = _____    29) 33 – _____ = 14    30) _____ – 25 = 10

31) 45 – _____ = 5    32) 34 – _____ = 1    33) 25 – _____ = 5

34) 28 – 17 = _____    35) _____ – 23 = 18    36) 49 – _____ = 20

37) 46 – _____ = 31    38) _____ – 15 = 21    39) 10 – 6 = _____

40) 7 – 5 = _____    41) 46 – 9 = _____    42) 36 – _____ = 21

43) 44 – 7 = _____    44) _____ – 40 = 1    45) _____ – 8 = 9

1) _____ − 11 = 10

2) _____ − 6 = 14

3) _____ − 12 = 9

4) 29 − 20 = _____

5) _____ − 16 = 21

6) _____ − 2 = 19

7) 34 − _____ = 20

8) 42 − _____ = 1

9) 29 − 28 = _____

10) _____ − 4 = 25

11) 9 − 7 = _____

12) 46 − _____ = 24

13) 21 − _____ = 6

14) 40 − _____ = 36

15) 34 − _____ = 15

16) _____ − 20 = 21

17) 31 − _____ = 30

18) 26 − _____ = 25

19) _____ − 3 = 41

20) _____ − 12 = 21

21) 48 − _____ = 24

22) 31 − _____ = 30

23) 49 − _____ = 9

24) _____ − 2 = 19

25) 39 − 2 = _____

26) 46 − _____ = 10

27) 47 − _____ = 23

28) 35 − _____ = 27

29) _____ − 4 = 13

30) _____ − 23 = 25

31) _____ − 17 = 4

32) _____ − 18 = 3

33) 20 − 1 = _____

34) 16 − _____ = 5

35) 32 − _____ = 28

36) 36 − 9 = _____

37) 31 − _____ = 15

38) 49 − _____ = 6

39) 38 − _____ = 10

40) _____ − 30 = 5

41) 30 − _____ = 29

42) 36 − 22 = _____

43) _____ − 33 = 5

44) _____ − 5 = 9

45) 7 − 2 = _____

1) 50 – _____ = 22     2) 35 – 28 = _____     3) 43 – 7 = _____

4) _____ – 46 = 0     5) 44 – _____ = 13     6) 49 – _____ = 28

7) 4 – 1 = _____     8) 40 – _____ = 37     9) _____ – 9 = 10

10) 45 – 23 = _____     11) 33 – _____ = 30     12) 43 – _____ = 38

13) 31 – 26 = _____     14) _____ – 27 = 6     15) 48 – 31 = _____

16) _____ – 6 = 17     17) 23 – _____ = 4     18) _____ – 1 = 13

19) 47 – _____ = 21     20) _____ – 2 = 16     21) _____ – 16 = 10

22) _____ – 43 = 4     23) 48 – 47 = _____     24) _____ – 8 = 25

25) _____ – 16 = 16     26) 38 – 2 = _____     27) _____ – 18 = 22

28) 14 – 10 = _____     29) _____ – 30 = 5     30) _____ – 12 = 15

31) _____ – 18 = 10     32) _____ – 24 = 4     33) 44 – _____ = 20

34) _____ – 17 = 10     35) _____ – 6 = 44     36) _____ – 3 = 20

37) 49 – 47 = _____     38) 20 – _____ = 11     39) 3 – 1 = _____

40) _____ – 4 = 42     41) 46 – _____ = 31     42) 38 – _____ = 23

43) 40 – _____ = 33     44) _____ – 9 = 35     45) 42 – _____ = 13

  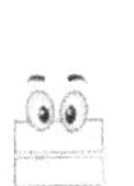 

1) 43 − _____ = 18     2) _____ − 22 = 10     3) 43 − 27 = _____

4) 22 − 19 = _____     5) 38 − _____ = 20     6) _____ − 32 = 13

7) 40 − _____ = 7     8) 28 − 27 = _____     9) _____ − 3 = 21

10) 37 − 18 = _____     11) _____ − 17 = 11     12) _____ − 14 = 34

13) 38 − 22 = _____     14) 20 − _____ = 9     15) _____ − 19 = 25

16) 40 − 12 = _____     17) 47 − _____ = 21     18) 8 − _____ = 3

19) 48 − 43 = _____     20) _____ − 39 = 5     21) 40 − _____ = 4

22) 38 − 21 = _____     23) _____ − 21 = 9     24) 49 − 7 = _____

25) _____ − 34 = 7     26) 48 − _____ = 22     27) _____ − 27 = 22

28) 14 − 11 = _____     29) 32 − _____ = 9     30) 40 − _____ = 32

31) 34 − 1 = _____     32) 47 − _____ = 38     33) _____ − 36 = 8

34) 30 − 19 = _____     35) 46 − _____ = 29     36) _____ − 1 = 40

37) _____ − 19 = 28     38) 15 − _____ = 4     39) 45 − _____ = 18

40) _____ − 7 = 4     41) _____ − 29 = 10     42) 40 − _____ = 37

43) _____ − 20 = 18     44) 43 − 22 = _____     45) _____ − 34 = 10

1) _____ − 11 = 31        2) 14 − _____ = 6        3) _____ − 27 = 3

4) 16 − 15 = _____        5) 17 − _____ = 11        6) 48 − _____ = 41

7) 36 − _____ = 35        8) _____ − 28 = 0        9) 6 − _____ = 3

10) 49 − _____ = 37        11) 44 − _____ = 27        12) 48 − 23 = _____

13) 33 − 21 = _____        14) 34 − _____ = 12        15) _____ − 4 = 4

16) 41 − _____ = 31        17) 46 − 36 = _____        18) 22 − _____ = 1

19) _____ − 18 = 15        20) 18 − 8 = _____        21) 32 − 6 = _____

22) 30 − 8 = _____        23) 23 − _____ = 0        24) 49 − 18 = _____

25) 5 − _____ = 3        26) 31 − _____ = 25        27) _____ − 11 = 9

28) 39 − _____ = 30        29) _____ − 19 = 9        30) _____ − 45 = 4

31) 33 − _____ = 25        32) _____ − 3 = 27        33) 43 − _____ = 23

34) _____ − 6 = 23        35) 42 − _____ = 19        36) _____ − 5 = 3

37) 29 − 26 = _____        38) 42 − _____ = 2        39) 18 − _____ = 3

40) _____ − 6 = 31        41) 35 − _____ = 1        42) _____ − 31 = 0

43) 22 − _____ = 8        44) _____ − 8 = 9        45) 47 − _____ = 27

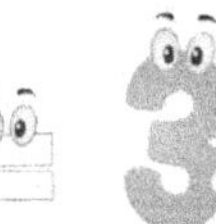

# Missing Number
# 0-100

1) ____ − 2 = 54

2) ____ − 25 = 44

3) 81 − 68 = ____

4) 93 − 76 = ____

5) 28 − 7 = ____

6) ____ − 18 = 52

7) ____ − 82 = 1

8) ____ − 74 = 12

9) 55 − ____ = 47

10) 31 − ____ = 23

11) 80 − ____ = 36

12) ____ − 7 = 89

13) 81 − ____ = 20

14) 56 − 7 = ____

15) 94 − ____ = 51

16) ____ − 14 = 60

17) 66 − ____ = 56

18) 85 − ____ = 83

19) 50 − ____ = 25

20) 43 − 19 = ____

21) ____ − 75 = 8

22) 49 − 10 = ____

23) ____ − 4 = 82

24) 95 − 16 = ____

25) ____ − 2 = 43

26) ____ − 81 = 17

27) ____ − 1 = 15

28) 41 − ____ = 21

29) 94 − ____ = 11

30) 34 − ____ = 5

31) ____ − 62 = 32

32) 63 − ____ = 54

33) ____ − 1 = 44

34) 51 − ____ = 20

35) 81 − ____ = 33

36) 22 − ____ = 20

37) ____ − 40 = 47

38) 63 − ____ = 7

39) ____ − 33 = 3

40) 68 − 41 = ____

41) ____ − 47 = 39

42) 46 − ____ = 20

43) 93 − ____ = 30

44) ____ − 57 = 6

45) 96 − ____ = 11

1) $99 - 9 = $ ____    2) $89 - 33 = $ ____    3) $74 - $ ____ $ = 56$

4) ____ $ - 44 = 11$    5) $97 - 92 = $ ____    6) ____ $ - 44 = 44$

7) ____ $ - 83 = 11$    8) $75 - 13 = $ ____    9) $39 - 4 = $ ____

10) $38 - $ ____ $ = 3$    11) ____ $ - 27 = 71$    12) $91 - $ ____ $ = 75$

13) $99 - $ ____ $ = 63$    14) $41 - 41 = $ ____    15) $84 - $ ____ $ = 27$

16) $85 - $ ____ $ = 82$    17) $91 - 67 = $ ____    18) $67 - $ ____ $ = 64$

19) $74 - $ ____ $ = 13$    20) $73 - 54 = $ ____    21) ____ $ - 44 = 17$

22) $86 - $ ____ $ = 25$    23) $67 - $ ____ $ = 61$    24) ____ $ - 16 = 80$

25) $65 - 15 = $ ____    26) $88 - $ ____ $ = 84$    27) $74 - $ ____ $ = 5$

28) ____ $ - 18 = 37$    29) $75 - 8 = $ ____    30) $43 - $ ____ $ = 40$

31) $51 - $ ____ $ = 25$    32) ____ $ - 2 = 5$    33) $63 - $ ____ $ = 1$

34) $87 - 79 = $ ____    35) ____ $ - 37 = 60$    36) $64 - $ ____ $ = 35$

37) $99 - $ ____ $ = 41$    38) $87 - 53 = $ ____    39) $81 - $ ____ $ = 58$

40) $28 - $ ____ $ = 9$    41) ____ $ - 27 = 59$    42) $53 - $ ____ $ = 19$

43) $58 - 58 = $ ____    44) ____ $ - 10 = 44$    45) ____ $ - 74 = 25$

1) _____ − 4 = 60      2) _____ − 12 = 36      3) 37 − _____ = 27

4) _____ − 16 = 70     5) _____ − 54 = 10      6) 89 − _____ = 6

7) _____ − 39 = 50     8) 65 − _____ = 37      9) 92 − 63 = _____

10) 48 − 44 = _____    11) 75 − _____ = 58     12) 38 − _____ = 21

13) _____ − 14 = 50    14) 68 − _____ = 34     15) 52 − 8 = _____

16) _____ − 67 = 5     17) 47 − _____ = 44     18) _____ − 53 = 37

19) _____ − 12 = 85    20) 89 − _____ = 79     21) _____ − 46 = 17

22) _____ − 59 = 18    23) 97 − _____ = 19     24) _____ − 33 = 14

25) 94 − _____ = 81    26) 68 − _____ = 22     27) 97 − 9 = _____

28) _____ − 32 = 31    29) 80 − _____ = 6      30) 89 − 47 = _____

31) 82 − 68 = _____    32) _____ − 45 = 5      33) _____ − 17 = 79

34) _____ − 10 = 65    35) _____ − 21 = 45     36) 89 − _____ = 18

37) 93 − _____ = 45    38) _____ − 75 = 18     39) _____ − 19 = 16

40) 85 − _____ = 50    41) _____ − 24 = 3      42) 79 − 30 = _____

43) 73 − 66 = _____    44) 44 − _____ = 1      45) 86 − _____ = 1

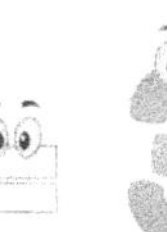

1) 66 − _____ = 38    2) 57 − 48 = _____    3) _____ − 10 = 53

4) 64 − _____ = 27    5) 54 − 29 = _____    6) 80 − 57 = _____

7) 19 − _____ = 10    8) 19 − 4 = _____    9) 78 − _____ = 10

10) 61 − _____ = 47    11) _____ − 34 = 59    12) _____ − 31 = 31

13) 46 − 2 = _____    14) 40 − _____ = 23    15) _____ − 45 = 26

16) _____ − 19 = 43    17) 23 − _____ = 10    18) 58 − _____ = 49

19) 63 − _____ = 51    20) 40 − 3 = _____    21) _____ − 17 = 73

22) 27 − _____ = 0    23) 100 − _____ = 89    24) _____ − 6 = 19

25) _____ − 20 = 51    26) 74 − 68 = _____    27) 80 − 31 = _____

28) 66 − _____ = 15    29) 65 − _____ = 51    30) 73 − _____ = 32

31) 62 − _____ = 7    32) 24 − 8 = _____    33) _____ − 1 = 56

34) _____ − 71 = 20    35) 73 − _____ = 55    36) 82 − _____ = 51

37) 46 − _____ = 3    38) 70 − _____ = 22    39) 55 − 22 = _____

40) 85 − _____ = 58    41) 75 − _____ = 17    42) _____ − 56 = 29

43) 83 − 23 = _____    44) 19 − 3 = _____    45) _____ − 41 = 3

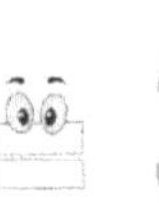

1) 83 – _____ = 54          2) _____ – 18 = 57          3) 74 – _____ = 38

4) 57 – 16 = _____          5) _____ – 6 = 24          6) _____ – 42 = 37

7) 90 – _____ = 49          8) 88 – 76 = _____          9) _____ – 34 = 45

10) 40 – _____ = 6          11) _____ – 9 = 57          12) _____ – 39 = 33

13) 89 – _____ = 69          14) 100 – _____ = 80          15) 58 – 44 = _____

16) 11 – _____ = 4          17) 42 – 13 = _____          18) 57 – _____ = 34

19) _____ – 18 = 79          20) 91 – 14 = _____          21) _____ – 5 = 21

22) _____ – 54 = 40          23) _____ – 31 = 4          24) 94 – _____ = 86

25) _____ – 4 = 3          26) 39 – _____ = 32          27) _____ – 10 = 25

28) _____ – 8 = 60          29) 69 – 58 = _____          30) 49 – _____ = 33

31) 75 – _____ = 39          32) 80 – _____ = 79          33) 75 – _____ = 12

34) _____ – 43 = 2          35) 83 – _____ = 36          36) 62 – _____ = 58

37) 16 – _____ = 4          38) 75 – 23 = _____          39) 84 – 19 = _____

40) _____ – 66 = 1          41) _____ – 39 = 12          42) _____ – 34 = 35

43) 65 – _____ = 50          44) 53 – 19 = _____          45) 96 – _____ = 60

1) 46 – _____ = 22

2) 95 – _____ = 90

3) _____ – 53 = 6

4) _____ – 16 = 30

5) 55 – _____ = 54

6) 92 – _____ = 62

7) 68 – 37 = _____

8) 88 – _____ = 39

9) _____ – 62 = 31

10) _____ – 35 = 5

11) 25 – _____ = 14

12) 13 – 12 = _____

13) _____ – 81 = 6

14) _____ – 24 = 31

15) 82 – _____ = 70

16) _____ – 5 = 93

17) _____ – 20 = 5

18) 33 – _____ = 24

19) _____ – 1 = 47

20) _____ – 32 = 59

21) 50 – _____ = 8

22) _____ – 31 = 12

23) 100 – 79 = _____

24) 53 – _____ = 25

25) _____ – 8 = 84

26) _____ – 24 = 46

27) _____ – 79 = 2

28) 17 – _____ = 8

29) 19 – _____ = 11

30) 95 – _____ = 17

31) _____ – 22 = 31

32) _____ – 71 = 11

33) _____ – 64 = 10

34) 71 – 47 = _____

35) _____ – 22 = 22

36) 42 – _____ = 7

37) 75 – _____ = 56

38) 95 – _____ = 73

39) _____ – 12 = 15

40) _____ – 24 = 5

41) 86 – 50 = _____

42) 76 – 53 = _____

43) 40 – _____ = 28

44) _____ – 27 = 57

45) _____ – 31 = 11

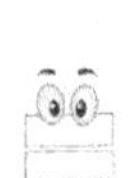

1) 87 − 46 = _____   2) _____ − 57 = 7   3) _____ − 45 = 24

4) 31 − _____ = 6   5) 65 − _____ = 14   6) _____ − 58 = 37

7) _____ − 82 = 16   8) 52 − _____ = 16   9) _____ − 3 = 51

10) 52 − 48 = _____   11) 88 − 53 = _____   12) _____ − 36 = 27

13) 24 − _____ = 14   14) _____ − 16 = 75   15) 83 − _____ = 37

16) 56 − _____ = 1   17) _____ − 71 = 6   18) _____ − 8 = 73

19) 46 − 30 = _____   20) 80 − 75 = _____   21) _____ − 18 = 10

22) 85 − 56 = _____   23) 57 − _____ = 9   24) 19 − 8 = _____

25) 57 − _____ = 29   26) 83 − 15 = _____   27) 32 − _____ = 3

28) 88 − _____ = 54   29) 99 − _____ = 43   30) _____ − 6 = 22

31) _____ − 53 = 32   32) 16 − 16 = _____   33) _____ − 4 = 92

34) _____ − 2 = 14   35) _____ − 52 = 18   36) _____ − 55 = 26

37) 52 − _____ = 25   38) _____ − 41 = 37   39) _____ − 38 = 36

40) 89 − 44 = _____   41) 76 − _____ = 65   42) _____ − 24 = 30

43) 100 − _____ = 55   44) _____ − 56 = 34   45) _____ − 33 = 38

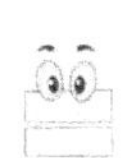

1) _____ − 18 = 1          2) _____ − 24 = 27          3) _____ − 35 = 42

4) _____ − 50 = 47         5) 45 − _____ = 43          6) _____ − 28 = 19

7) _____ − 35 = 56         8) _____ − 35 = 59          9) 67 − 48 = _____

10) _____ − 40 = 58        11) _____ − 31 = 5          12) _____ − 18 = 74

13) _____ − 2 = 72         14) _____ − 19 = 63         15) 24 − 7 = _____

16) 56 − _____ = 25        17) _____ − 55 = 38         18) 34 − _____ = 6

19) _____ − 34 = 4         20) _____ − 64 = 34         21) _____ − 27 = 70

22) 6 − 6 = _____          23) 69 − 40 = _____         24) _____ − 1 = 70

25) 59 − 20 = _____        26) 84 − 72 = _____         27) 98 − _____ = 65

28) _____ − 50 = 27        29) _____ − 5 = 30          30) _____ − 32 = 5

31) _____ − 46 = 36        32) _____ − 54 = 12         33) 41 − _____ = 33

34) 50 − _____ = 9         35) _____ − 28 = 68         36) 97 − _____ = 74

37) 77 − _____ = 77        38) 62 − _____ = 17         39) 89 − _____ = 63

40) _____ − 82 = 12        41) _____ − 8 = 75          42) _____ − 13 = 78

43) 97 − _____ = 12        44) 87 − _____ = 81         45) 62 − _____ = 10

1) 89 − 83 = _____    2) 92 − _____ = 64    3) _____ − 35 = 38

4) 46 − _____ = 13    5) 24 − 8 = _____    6) 85 − _____ = 31

7) 79 − _____ = 11    8) _____ − 90 = 2    9) 88 − _____ = 29

10) _____ − 91 = 8    11) 94 − _____ = 79    12) _____ − 14 = 20

13) _____ − 40 = 35    14) 13 − 4 = _____    15) 75 − _____ = 17

16) _____ − 63 = 11    17) _____ − 89 = 10    18) _____ − 60 = 14

19) _____ − 44 = 12    20) 82 − _____ = 28    21) 80 − _____ = 32

22) 37 − _____ = 20    23) 63 − 60 = _____    24) _____ − 2 = 54

25) 33 − _____ = 29    26) 87 − _____ = 24    27) 70 − _____ = 6

28) _____ − 28 = 4    29) 78 − _____ = 47    30) _____ − 52 = 3

31) _____ − 42 = 1    32) 66 − _____ = 55    33) 87 − _____ = 50

34) 67 − 44 = _____    35) _____ − 5 = 17    36) 56 − 30 = _____

37) _____ − 65 = 13    38) 99 − _____ = 17    39) 72 − _____ = 37

40) _____ − 10 = 57    41) 75 − _____ = 59    42) 50 − _____ = 39

43) _____ − 12 = 53    44) 49 − 40 = _____    45) 77 − _____ = 22

1) $96 - \underline{\hspace{2em}} = 59$  2) $96 - 48 = \underline{\hspace{2em}}$  3) $73 - \underline{\hspace{2em}} = 63$

4) $76 - 2 = \underline{\hspace{2em}}$  5) $78 - 3 = \underline{\hspace{2em}}$  6) $\underline{\hspace{2em}} - 47 = 6$

7) $\underline{\hspace{2em}} - 44 = 3$  8) $27 - 26 = \underline{\hspace{2em}}$  9) $\underline{\hspace{2em}} - 20 = 68$

10) $84 - \underline{\hspace{2em}} = 5$  11) $69 - \underline{\hspace{2em}} = 50$  12) $82 - 44 = \underline{\hspace{2em}}$

13) $58 - \underline{\hspace{2em}} = 18$  14) $71 - 26 = \underline{\hspace{2em}}$  15) $34 - 21 = \underline{\hspace{2em}}$

16) $82 - 72 = \underline{\hspace{2em}}$  17) $89 - 25 = \underline{\hspace{2em}}$  18) $\underline{\hspace{2em}} - 4 = 19$

19) $\underline{\hspace{2em}} - 27 = 1$  20) $26 - \underline{\hspace{2em}} = 26$  21) $\underline{\hspace{2em}} - 3 = 33$

22) $93 - \underline{\hspace{2em}} = 2$  23) $\underline{\hspace{2em}} - 17 = 63$  24) $\underline{\hspace{2em}} - 24 = 18$

25) $\underline{\hspace{2em}} - 45 = 4$  26) $42 - 7 = \underline{\hspace{2em}}$  27) $65 - 50 = \underline{\hspace{2em}}$

28) $98 - \underline{\hspace{2em}} = 26$  29) $94 - 83 = \underline{\hspace{2em}}$  30) $92 - \underline{\hspace{2em}} = 16$

31) $\underline{\hspace{2em}} - 59 = 32$  32) $25 - 11 = \underline{\hspace{2em}}$  33) $\underline{\hspace{2em}} - 48 = 34$

34) $\underline{\hspace{2em}} - 9 = 29$  35) $70 - \underline{\hspace{2em}} = 26$  36) $67 - \underline{\hspace{2em}} = 24$

37) $\underline{\hspace{2em}} - 48 = 7$  38) $87 - \underline{\hspace{2em}} = 38$  39) $84 - 58 = \underline{\hspace{2em}}$

40) $\underline{\hspace{2em}} - 36 = 47$  41) $95 - \underline{\hspace{2em}} = 78$  42) $97 - \underline{\hspace{2em}} = 41$

43) $70 - 25 = \underline{\hspace{2em}}$  44) $47 - 14 = \underline{\hspace{2em}}$  45) $67 - \underline{\hspace{2em}} = 25$